D1066131

Volumes in Preparation

Olga Preobrazhenskaya, a biography, by Elvira Roné, *translated by Fernau Hall*

Ballerina, a biography of Violette Verdy, by Victoria Huckenpahler

The Bournonville School (in four volumes), including music and notation, by Kirsten Ralov, *introduction by Walter Terry*

I Was There, by Walter Terry, *compiled and edited by Andrew Wentink, introduction by Anna Kisselgoff*

The Bennington Years: 1934-1942, a chronology and source book, by Sali Ann Kriegsman

The Art and Practice of Ballet Accompanying (in two volumes), by Elizabeth Sawyer Brady

The Ballet Russe (in four volumes), edited by George Jackson

Imperial Dancer, a biography of Felia Doubrovska, by Victoria Huckenpahler

Antony Tudor, a biography, by Fernau Hall

Dancer's Diary, by Dennis Wayne, *introduction by Joanne Woodward*

Marius Petipa, by A. Nekhendzi, *translated by Tamara Bering Sunguroff*

On Tap Dancing

On Tap Dancing

PAUL DRAPER

Edited and compiled by
FRAN AVALLONE

Marcel Dekker, Inc.   New York and Basel

Library of Congress Cataloging in Publication Data

Draper, Paul, 1909-
    On tap dancing.

    (The Dance program ; v. 8)
    1. Tap dancing – Collected works. I. Avallone,
Fran. II. Title. III. Series.
GV1794.D68   793.3'24   77-17886
ISBN 0-8247-6650-4

The articles in this book are reprinted courtesy of *Dance Magazine*: **1** September–
December, 1960; **2** January–May, 1957; **3** April–May, 1959; **4** March–April,
1958; **5** December, 1958; **6** April–May, 1960; **7** June–July, 1958; **8** May–
June, 1962; **9** December, 1962 – February, 1963; **10** November, 1957 – February,
1958; **11** October–November, 1958; **12** January–February, 1961; **13** October–
December, 1961; **14** June, 1961, March, 1959, August, 1958, June, 1959; **15** December, 1959 – February, 1960; **16** April, 1955; **17** November, 1954 – January,
1955; **18** February–March, 1955; **19** August, 1955; **20** October–December,
1956; **21** February, 1956; **22** March, 1960, February, 1962; **23** July, 1961;
24 May, 1961; **25** August–November, 1962.

*Photographs of Paul Draper on the cover and frontispiece are reproduced by courtesy of
Lincoln Center Dance Library.*

MARCEL DEKKER, INC.
270 Madison Avenue, New York, New York 10016

Current printing (last digit):
10   9   8   7   6   5   4   3   2   1

PRINTED IN THE UNITED STATES OF AMERICA

Preface

I wrote these articles for *Dance Magazine* during the years 1954 through 1963. They were not intended to teach the uninitiated, nor in fact to "teach" in any technical sense at any level. Rather, they are an attempt to share some of my experiences on the stage and in the rehearsal hall.

I have spent many thousands of hours in both places. All but a few of those hours have been filled with wonder and joy— wonder at the inexhaustible challenge of dance as a way to live, and joy at being part of the process. Of course one never succeeds in attaining one's dream of really mastering the art, but one does achieve some measure of control over oneself, and I have attempted to describe some of the things that have happened to me along that never-ending way. Also, I have tried to pass on some of what I have learned, and to give advice and hints which I hope will be of value to both students and teachers. Tap dancers who use this book will encounter some steps that are very basic along with some rather difficult ones. It is always hard to describe physical actions in words, particularly where those actions have to be coordinated with exact rhythmic patterns, and if I have failed to make some things clear it is entirely my responsibility. I am grateful to Fran Avallone for her encouragement and assistance in collecting and preparing the material for publication.

Although this is not a textbook it is most certainly a book about tap dancing and it is, I hope, a way of communicating to you some of the excitement generated by the hard but loving work that every dancer knows so well.

Paul Draper

Introduction

When I was seven years old, my mother took me to a matinee performance by Paul Draper and Larry Adler at Town Hall. It was during the Easter school vacation and the audience was filled with mothers and children. That afternoon I fell in love with tap dancing—especially Paul Draper's dancing—and from then on there was no doubt in my mind what I was going to be when I grew up.

I pestered my parents until I was allowed to take lessons at a local school but my goal was to study someday with Paul Draper and learn to dance the way he did. Nine years later an ad appeared in *Dance Magazine* announcing that Paul would be teaching, and I was first in line to sign up. It was the answer to my dreams to be able to study with this genius of tap dancing.

Paul Draper was born in Florence, Italy, in 1909. When he was two years old the family moved to London and when he was six the Drapers came to the United States. At age 17, after running away from school to dig ditches in Woodstock, New York, Paul was persuaded by his aunt, Ruth Draper, the monologist, to take an engineering course at the Polytechnic Institute, but he only stayed one year. He later worked at various jobs; for a short time as the assistant music critic on the *New York World* and then briefly as an instructor at an Arthur Murray dance school where he learned a time step from one of the other teachers. He made up some tap dances and began his career in 1931 in London. Returning to this country in the early thirties, he performed at Radio City Music Hall and other theaters in New York City, and for years in night clubs around the country he did his act on top of a small round marble-topped pedestal.

Some years later he realized that he had to learn how to dance, so he studied with Anatole Vilzak and Anatole Oboukhoff at the School of American Ballet. In 1939 Paul teamed up with Larry Adler, the harmonica virtuoso, and they gave their first recital in Santa Barbara. For years they were an extremely popular attraction on the national concert scene, giving 60 to 70 performances a year.

In 1949 they became the target of the Blacklist because of a Connecticut housewife who wanted to cancel their concert in her hometown. They filed a libel suit against the woman on the basis of a letter accusing them of pro-Communist activities. The suit ended in a hung jury, but because of it Paul and Larry were unable to find employment. Larry Adler moved to London where he has lived ever since, and Paul moved to Switzerland with his family. He gave concerts in Europe, toured Israel in 1951, and returned to the United States in 1954.

Besides teaching, Paul gave concerts around the country during the late fifties and early sixties. He appeared on Broadway, once with Ruth Draper, and gave many performances at the 92nd Street YMHA. Since the fall of 1969 Paul has been an Andrew Mellon Professor of Drama at Carnegie Mellon University in Pittsburgh.

Paul married Heidi Vosseler, a ballerina in the American Ballet Company, in June 1941 and they now have three daughters, Susan, Pamela, and Kate. Pamela and Kate are in the performing arts and Susan manages a restaurant in New York City.

On June 15, 1975, Paul and Larry Adler were reunited at Carnegie Hall. The audience was packed with former students, friends, and admirers. I had not seen Paul perform for quite a few years and his artistry and genius brought tears to my eyes. Watching him dance is a great experience and the concert brought memories flooding back of the other times I had seen him perform, the classes I took, and the after-class cups of hot chocolate.

While watching Paul and Larry Adler, I thought of the stacks of *Dance Magazine* sitting in my closet containing articles written by Paul. For many years he did a monthly column and I thought of all the dance teachers and students who hadn't seen them, and that's how this book came to be.

There are many people involved in the production of the book whom I would like to thank: Pat O'Connor for his advice; Lincoln Center Dance Library for the use of the photographs from their files; Frank Derbas for reproducing the photos; my husband, Michael, for his encouragement; *Dance Magazine* for their permission to use the articles; and most of all, Paul Draper for his talent, his artistry, his friendship, and the happiness his dancing has given me.

Fran Avallone

Contents

1 Tap dancing

I love to dance. I love being a tap dancer, and I love doing tap dancing.

But I am ashamed of most of the tap dancing I see at schools and conventions. I am ashamed of how it is taught, how it is performed, and how it is generally considered as a form of dance expression.

I have taught at several conventions and have had an opportunity to be an eye-and-ear witness of the facts which have led to the above conclusions. This does not mean that there are not many very sincere and hard-working tap teachers. There are. It means that because of inadequate training and lack of demand they have developed only the lowest level of their possibilities.

Tap dancing is a beautiful and exciting form of dance. There is no valid reason why it should be relegated to amateur shows, or disregarded altogether as if unfit to be taught, learned or performed.

At one convention I received a letter from an especially serious teacher who is concerned about this subject. Her letter asked me many questions which I would like to answer now.

Anyone who thinks tap dancing is of the same value as baton-twirling or rope-skipping can stop here, for both she and I consider tap dance an art.

The first question is: *How do you think the method of teaching tap dancing can be improved in schools?*

It can be improved by teaching students how to dance instead of teaching them routines. In my opinion an instructor whose class consists of working on routines has no business teaching dancing at all. Not every student can learn to dance—perhaps very few can—whereas almost anybody can learn a

1

routine, if it is simple enough. Very few students learn how to dance no matter how you teach them. Those who can should have a chance to, and they never will if they learn only routines.

Before beginning to study tap dancing a student must have some sense of coordination, body control and rhythm. The first two can best be acquired by studying ballet, and rhythm can best be acquired by studying music. So, I would insist on at least a year of ballet before starting to tap dance, and at least six months of rhythmic training during the same period. Now how long is a year? It isn't once a week for sporadic periods, with a four-month vacation thrown in. It is, at beginner level, at least twice a week, preferably three times, for an hour or an hour and a half each lesson. That's 104 to 156 hours a year. Say 125 hours in ballet and about 60 in rhythmic training. That is not very much, though I meet people who claim to have been studying six or seven years who haven't spent much more time than that and consider themselves at practically professional level.

The student should now be able to walk neatly, raise an arm with an opposite leg, do a pas de bourrée and count to four in time with a simple piece of music, or even to three if the need arises. This student knows the difference between front and back and right and left, knows how to do a pirouette, though perhaps cannot perform one yet, and can jump high enough to do a changement without bending the knees and with pointed feet. This student can move around a medium-size floor space with grace and flexibility, not necessarily doing specific steps. Now aware of posture and alignment, she can begin to study tap dance.

This is the first step in improving the method of teaching tap in schools. It eliminates the outstanding mistake of attempting to learn to tap dance without any other dance training, the inevitable result of which is to flail around like an intoxicated chicken.

The next step is to consider tap dancing seriously and to teach it methodically by beginning with exercises instead of with steps. It is essential that they be practiced diligently and that they be done with arm and body movement at the same time.

As an example, consider shuffles. Almost every tap teacher I have seen teaches a student to throw a shuffle with a loose ankle and make two sounds. This results in a student learning to make two sounds all right, but always the same two sounds. The sounds made with a shuffle should be controllable to any shape and speed you desire. This can be accomplished only through thousands of repetitions of brushing outward from sur le coup de pied and inward to sur le coup de pied with a straight, pointed foot. Front, side and back. This is not how you *dance* a shuffle. This is how you learn to develop and control the muscles which enable you to dance a shuffle.

As with shuffles, you must develop and control the muscles which enable you to do all tap steps. Let it be clearly understood that doing a certain step over and over does not necessarily teach you how to do it—or to improve it if you already know how to do it. A shot putter does many exercises besides putting the shot. High jumpers lift weights, and pianists take exercises for their arms, wrists and fingers which are not directly related to playing the piano.

One of the best exercises for learning to do a pull-back is to stand on one foot, with the other foot in sur le coup de pied, and slowly beat the floor as if driving a nail. Do this with a controlled down-stroke and a controlled up-stroke without moving your leg. Move the foot from the ankle only. Lift the foot up as high as you can, and hit the floor as hard as you can. Do it until the long muscle on the outside of your shin bone can stand it no longer. Vary the speed, but never let it become a nerve tap. If you do this often enough you will soon be able to do a pull-back from the ball of the foot as if you were doing a simple back slap. You will no longer have to stamp down on the flat foot in order to feel a secure starting point for the pull-back.

Who wants to do this exercise long enough to achieve results? Only those who want to learn to tap dance in a meaningful way. And "meaningful" is commercial as well as communicative. Believe me, the better you dance the more money you make.

There are two very good exercises for learning wings. One is to rotate the foot from the ankle without moving any other part

of the leg. Do this both inward and outward until you feel too
tired to continue. The other is to stand beside a wall, as if you
were at the barre, and press the outside edge of the front of
your foot against the base of the wall, where it meets the floor.
Do this with a straight leg. Press and relax, press and relax. A
wing is not a difficult step, and is only made to seem so by
teachers who can't do them. It is about as hard as any entrechat
quatre is in ballet. It is a very valuable step—far more so in tap
than the entrechat quatre is in ballet—and can be done as fluently and effortlessly as you do slaps. It is also a very small step
which, since it is done on one foot, leaves great scope for large
movements of the other leg, the arms and the body. Don't let
anyone tell you a wing is an advanced or difficult step. It just
isn't. It is hard to learn, but not to do. It is hard to learn to
stand up straight, too. And so it is with any technique.

The problem lies more properly in the attitudes about tap
dancing than in how excellently the steps are performed. So
long as teachers, students and dancers go about it as if it were
just for kiddies, so it will be. So long as a certain embarrassment
underlies whatever outward manifestation the dancer employs,
then so will an audience feel embarrassment. The audience will
perhaps not recognize their reaction as such, and will applaud or
giggle as the case may be, but they will not be moved. If you
do not wish to move an audience, then you should find a pro-
fession where there is no obligation to do so. There is a growing
need for physicists, doctors and many other skilled and difficult
forms of human endeavor that make no demand that a beautiful
relationship between an artist and a group of strangers be created.
Choose one. But if you want to be a dancer, then accept with
awareness and pride the fact that good steps and a cute personality are no more germane to a dancer than a sharp scalpel and a
soothing bedside manner are to a surgeon. Valuable assets, yes.
But they do not guarantee great achievements.

Dancing isn't like a new skirt and sweater or a necktie, it isn't
something you can put on and take off, it isn't something you wear.
It is your whole self, your way of living, and your expression of
that way. If you don't think it's worth that much, then don't do it.

I am excluding for the moment that large body of people who want only to keep physically fit and take up dancing as less monotonous and boring than setting-up exercises.

I maintain that the first step toward improving the method of tap dancing in schools is to change their attitude toward tap dancing.

The second question I was asked is: *What do you mean by a "primitive" method of counting?*

At risk of boring many of you, I should like to review what I consider to be the faults of the counting method now generally used for tap dancing, and what I think should be done to improve it.

First, to define terms. Counting in any fashion is a much more mysterious process than you might imagine. Just think of a language without numbers and then try to devise a way of denoting how many objects there are in any group of objects. For "one" it is not difficult to say "this" or "that." For a group we will allow you "several." But to define the difference between six and seven is a considerable intellectual process. Try it. Some tribes still exist that have no word for more than three. Think about it.

It is likely that the first concept of enumerating a sequence of events arose from the contemplation of a beating heart. Someone got tired of saying beat, beat, beat, beat, and thought up one, two, three, four. (We have now, of course, returned to beat, beat!)

In our society, music was one of the first subjects to be made more understandable by the science of counting. At first it resulted in great confusion. The psychology of man made him like counting in twos and threes, and he regarded triple time as perfect because it corresponded to the Holy Trinity. Out of confusion and a mild neurosis, we have, however, devised a practical system of communicating the temporal, metrical and rhythmic ideas of a composer to a performer and an audience. Not so for the tap dancer, unfortunately. Anyone who would like to notate a tap routine for an age level beyond kindergarten is doomed to failure, or to such a morass of explanation that one's feet will never emerge from the swamp. A music student at almost any level can read and produce rhythms that are beyond the capacity of tap dancers to make readable.

Let us consider some examples. In tap notation one can count quarter notes—1, 2, 3, 4; eighth notes—1 and 2 and 3 and 4 and; eighth-note triplets—1 and a 2 and a 3 and a 4 and a; and sixteenth notes—1 ay and a 2 ay and a, etc. Now you can shift the basic value of the 1, 2, 3, 4 to eighth notes or even to sixteenths, and thereby increase the divisibility of a bar of music, but you will also, as I shall show, run into so many words of explanation as to nullify the absorption powers of the reader. A greater limitation by far is the inherent ambiguity of using the symbol "a" to mean two different time values. In 1 and a 2 and a, etc., the "a" stands for one third of a quarter note. In 1 ay and a 2 ay and a, etc., the "a" stands for a sixteenth note. The difference that should exist between these values can flavor the whole feeling of a dance, and it is not clearly expressible in tap notation. It is perfectly clear to any high school drummer in a pick-up band—I resent the fact that a dancer does not have the same exact framework of reference. Suppose you want a dancer to do slaps, and you write the rhythm: a 1, a 2, a 3, a 4. Will he think of the "a" in 1 ay and a, or the "a" in 1 and a? Perhaps you don't think there is much difference. Just do it both ways and you'll see. Suppose you want to indicate half-note triplets, which make a rhythm of three against four and are very valuable in any jazz number. It can be done by writing: step on 1, step on the "and" after 2, and step on the "a" before 4 where the "a" is that of 1 and a 2 etc. Don't you think it would be easier to write half-note triplets as they would be written for a drummer?

Or take the case of grace notes, which in tap dancing are called the up-beat. Let's say the up-beat has five sounds in it. I suppose you could write "there are five sounds before 1," but it is clumsy and graceless to do this. Take a step like: stamp L on 1, shuffle R, pull back L, land R, L toe in back, drop R heel, L ball heel forward, R ball heel forward, stamp L on 2. The first stamp is held for the value of a sixteenth note. How do you write out the next eleven sounds, using the conventional method? A drummer could reproduce the desired effect with a glance at his music. What is so special about a drummer? He can read music.

I suggest that all dance students, or at least all teachers, learn to do the same. A few hours of study and a few weeks of application is all that would be necessary to follow a drum part. You don't have to learn a melodic line—just the rhythm. I think you would find that you no longer had to rely on the naively basic patterns of sound that are so much used today. I think your whole rhythmic imagination would begin to soar like a bird, and so might you.

The next question I was asked is: *How old should a student be to start studying tap or any other form of dancing*? This question has been asked ever since dancing schools began.

The problem involves several things that must be considered before an answer can be given: (1) Does "how old" refer to time alone, or to physical and psychological growth as well? (2) Is the school dedicated to creating and developing dancers, or to giving recitals and achieving social and economic status in the community? (3) Are the parents interested in the child having a future as a dancer, or acquiring at least some semblance of physical grace and coordination—or is dancing school primarily a means of finding free time for themselves?

It is known that children do not develop at the same rate. Some of us seem to be born mature, or even old, while others never grow much beyond the emotional level of a ten-year-old. Physiques also grow at unequal rates, and boys mature physically quite differently from girls. There are, however, certain constants in bone and connective tissue formation which develop to a certain strain resistance at a fairly similar rate in all normal bodies. While joints and ligaments are forming, they may be bent like the proverbial twig toward a full realization of their potential. It must be kept in mind that the potential varies. Some of us are more flexible than others no matter what kind of training we have. Joints and ligaments must not be strained beyond their capacities, even if this seems fairly easy to do—as it will in a young body.

What constitutes a strain beyond capacity? First and fore-
most is standing on point, with or without toe shoes, before the
joints and ligaments are ready to accept the pressures this involves. This readiness generally occurs between eleven and thir-
teen years of age in girls—provided they have had at least several
years of sound preliminary training in ballet. Boys, due to a
fortunate combination of esthetic and psychological factors,
never have to contend with this problem.

You will note we have spoken of joints and ligaments. Muscles are somewhat different. It is difficult to harm a muscle as
such. Muscles respond wonderfully to exercise at almost any age
so long as the movements do not involve undue strain on skeletal
structures. An example of such an exercise is the grand battement. Here the thigh muscles may become sore and stiff, but
they will not be harmed. The only strain is on the joints and
bones of the supporting leg, and in this case it is not severe. On
the other hand, the relatively simple exercise of standing in a
perfectly turned out first position, where frictional contact with
the floor enables one to hold a position that the leg muscles
alone would not be able to do, can cause irreparable damage to
the ankle, knee and hip joints.

There is no space to go into all the movements of dance
exercise and divide them into muscle strain and ligament–joint
strain. If you are in doubt, ask an orthopedist, and keep in
mind that medical science in this field deals more with the rest-
ing than the active body. In all events avoid the spectacular and
the amazing. No amount of applause at age six is worth the possibility of chronically sore ankles, knees and lower backs later
on.

The second part of the question is easy to answer and difficult to do anything about if the answer is that the school is not
devoted to creating and developing dancers. Very often it is the
only school in the area, and you're stuck with it no matter
what. If you are fortunate, your schools will sincerely try to put
learning to dance ahead of showing off.

This leads to the last part of the question, the parents' attitude towards a dancing school. If you seriously want to be

relieved of some of your responsibility of bringing up your children, then it makes no difference what sort of school you send them to. You will be relieved, and that will be that. It makes no difference in this case what age they are when they start, and whatever happens will happen to you as much as to your children.

If you are really interested in the physical and emotional development of your child, then you will make an effort to see to it that the school is a good one. It will train your child to be able to comprehend, at least, the excitement and beauty of communication and expression that is part of dancing. It can lead your child to begin to understand emotional reality as opposed to gingerbread frippery. In this sort of school nothing but enrichment of growth and substance can result even if the student never dances a step professionally. In a sentence, dear parents, it's your baby.

2 Basic principles

For beginners

Very often beginners don't lift their feet enough when they shift their weight. The ball change is done almost without perceptible movement and consequently it is uncertain on which foot the next step begins. A shuffle is often a flat scuff, and a hop is barely detached from the floor.

Exaggerate these movements when you are learning them. Only by doing this will your neuro-muscular responses become well enough trained to enable you to dance with speed and strength later on. Don't try to emulate the feather-fast movements of your advanced brethren. Pick up your feet.

For intermediates

Move!

Don't pay so much attention to your feet. You know how to use them by this time, and you should be concentrating on broader lines of your dancing. When you do wings, the winging foot should be your least concern. Its movement is very small. Study the non-winging leg, the arms, head and shoulders. In tap turns think of the turn, and in jumps, of the jump. Go someplace with every step. Too many intermediates become hypnotized by the sound of their feet and begin dancing inwardly instead of opening up. Move!

For advanced dancers

Don't dance so quickly.

As your skills increase it is hard not to show them all the time. You often begin to practice at your top speed. You are so sure of what the sounds should be that you hear them that way no matter what you are really doing. But the better you are the more important it is to practice slowly.

Articulate every sound and every movement in a conscious and deliberate fashion. Great speed depends largely on nervous tension, and very often muscles deteriorate as a result of it. A very good dancer should dance like a beginner for a certain period every day. Slaps, shuffles, pull-backs, ball-heels and wings are especially likely to become worse if they are always done fast. Turns become blurred and line vanishes. So slow down to fly high. Not so fast and you'll get there.

The basics

Very few tap dancers seem to have learned the basic steps in tap dancing. They often went ahead to advanced steps and routines before having mastered fundamentals.

At risk of boring conscientious dancers, the basic steps are: steps, brushes, hops, slaps, shuffles, cramp-rolls, toe-taps, pull-backs and wings. These are the basic steps with which one makes sounds in tap dancing. Being able to do them perfectly does not mean you are a good tap dancer—you still have to learn to move, jump, turn and be someone on a stage. But if you can't do these basic steps, you will never be a good tap dancer no matter how well you dance.

The danger lies in that they appear to be so simple that their difficulty is seldom appreciated. Their appearance is very deceptive.

The step

Anybody can step. Right, left, right, left. Ball of the foot. Leg slightly bent. Ankle responsive to your weight and placement of your foot. The difficulty lies in making perfectly equal sounds with each step. If the ball of the foot makes contact with the floor so that one edge of the tap strikes before the weight is transferred you will not produce a clean tap. If you have sharply edged taps, which you shouldn't, you will make a double sound. If you land too far back on your foot, most of the sound will be muffled, sometimes it will be silent. If the heel drops unintentionally it will blur the tap; if you land too far forward near the tip of the tap, the tap will slide and you will produce a slight scraping sound. You must make contact firmly with the exact center of the tap. You must be able to do this from soft to loud at will. You must find out how softly you can step before you make no sound at all, and then try to maintain that level for a series of steps. You should be able to change directions sharply and at speed without changing the sound level of the steps. Then you must be able to change the sound level at will from soft to loud so that you can put accents wherever you want them.

None of this is easy and it is all worth practicing a great deal. If you can really control the quality and volume of every sound you make when you do a series of small steps you have made one very big step forward in your tap dancing education.

The brush

This is another step that appears to be of such essential simplicity that many dancers never work at it as diligently as they should. A brush consists of a quick movement of the leg to the front, the side or the back during which the foot makes contact with the floor for as short a time as is needed to produce a tap. As it makes contact it is flexed to a good strong point. It is not a scrape. You can avoid scraping by developing the speed with which your foot moves downwards to the floor and your leg moves to its straightened position. You should learn to do this

softly or with a strong accent, and singly or in succession. It
isn't easy. It is especially useful in the beginning of a jump or at
the end of a rhythmic pattern. A valuable exercise for developing
a clean, fast brush is to lift the foot about three or four inches
off the floor and literally beat the boards as if you were driving
a nail. Do this without moving the leg. (Also helpful for nerve
taps.)

All these things may sound obvious to some dancers. They
are the lucky ones. It is so wonderful that a human being can
stand up straight and walk, let alone dance, that most of us fail
to appreciate it. A reexamination of the obvious can be both
humbling and exalting. It can also improve your dancing.

Hops

Anybody can hop. But you would be surprised at how many
dancers make a mess of it. As in stepping it is essential to land
in the center of the tap on the ball of the foot. The heel must
not touch the floor and the hop must be straight up and down.
Now even to stand on one foot means a slight displacement of
the body in order to keep the hips even and not fall over from
the pull of the weight of the unsupported leg. It is in fact a
very complicated muscular feat to stand up on both feet without falling. We are so accustomed to it that we don't notice it.
To stand on one foot is almost miraculous—ask your doctor.
Many muscles are making continuous compensatory movements.
Help them by being aware of them. Don't just lean to the side
to balance—try to stand as straight as you can. Balance through
the ankle, the knee, the hip, the pelvis and the spine.

All that just to hop? Yes, and more. Now you have to control the height of the hop and the loudness of the landing. At
speed, say in fast hop shuffles, the hop is only about a quarter
of an inch off the floor. It is higher at slow tempos, though one
stays on the floor longer between hops so that it is not exactly
proportional.

By all odds the most important factor is to be sure the heel
remains in the air. If your calf muscles are weak or lazy you
will sometimes find it dropping to mar the clean sound, as it
can in "steps."

Slaps

A slap is really a combination of the first part of a brush and a step. There are forward slaps, back slaps and side slaps. It is a simple basic step, but the wise and wary know it has pitfalls. Chief among these is the fact that it is very easy to make different, unintentional rhythms when you use the slap in various directions. Next comes the ease with which a scraping sound can creep in where only a sharp tap should venture. And lastly there is the ease with which superfluous foot and leg movements can waste needed energy and destroy good line.

We will begin in reverse order to explain how to avoid these pitfalls. In doing slaps be sure not to move the leg farther forward than you are going to step with it. When you have lifted it and brushed forward to make the first sound of the slap, be sure that your next forward movement continues forward until you make final contact with the floor and shift your weight onto the slapping foot. It is very easy to let the impetus of the brush carry the leg farther ahead than you step, which means that in order to make contact with the floor you must move the leg backwards. Avoid this.

In back slaps the tendency is to swing the leg forward before beginning the brush to the back. Be sure that all your leg movement is directed backwards as your foot rises from the floor to begin the back slap. Then take care not to swing the leg farther back than is necessary before you step onto it.

Side slaps, depending on whether the leg is moving outward or inward, partake of the nature of both forward and back slaps. Figure out why for yourselves.

The scraping sound, in all directions, can be avoided by being sure the ankle raises the ball of the foot high enough before each slap and lowers it at a sharp angle rather than a gliding one and then raises it again before the step. This must be done whether the slaps are done almost in place or in long stretched-out movements.

Now for the variations in rhythm—the unintended ones that so easily mar good slaps. Slaps can be done in many rhythms. The most common is: and 1, and 2, and 3 and so forth. That can also be done: 1 and, 2 and; and in triplets; a 1, and a 2, and a 3, and a 4. Whichever way you count them it is important to be sure that you produce the desired sound whether they are done forwards, backwards, or sideways. You must ever be the master of your tap sounds and refuse to let the exigencies of direction and gravity dictate a flat-footed clump when there should be a feathered up-beat.

Shuffles

For many tap dancers the shuffle is not just a basic step—it is *the* basic step. They believe that if they can do shuffles with hops or with steps, they are well on the way to being dancers. This is far from the truth. Shuffles are important as a tool with which to build a tap structure and no more. And they are usually the worst performed of all basic steps.

A shuffle consists of brush forward and a brush back: 1, 2. The thigh moves the leg into the chosen position—to the front, the side, or to the back—and the brushes are done with the lower leg and the ankle. It is not to be done with a "thrown" or "flung" motion, like wringing your hands in despair. It is a controlled movement which can be done at any desired speed or rhythm. With practice the shuffle becomes a very small movement in which the ankle plays a larger part than the lower leg. When learning it the lower leg moves considerably. This movement becomes less and less until finally a shuffle is accomplished with about three inches of foot travel out and in, plus a very definite dropping of the ankle to make tap contact with the floor on the outward and inward brush. For clarity this contact must be positive and as short as possible. For rhythm you must be able to make an accent on either the outward or the inward brush, or make both sounds equal. It is very good practice to do a sequence of step-shuffles or hop-shuffles in the following rhythms; either double or triple: 1 and 2, 3 and 4, or 1 and a 2 and a 3 and a 4, or 1 a and a 2 a and a 3, etc. Do these at all possible speeds, and make sure you are aware of the accented beats as they change from one part of the step to another.

I must add that the word "shuffle" bears no resemblance to the step it symbolizes. Take care not to shuffle when you "shuffle."

Cramp-rolls

This designation covers a multitude of sins and steps. We'll begin with the step. A cramp-roll is basically a combination of steps and heel drops, such as step, step, heel, heel, or step, heel, step, heel. The first pattern is most useful for a landing from a small jump, either in fifth position or with the feet parallel, as in skiing. Great care must be taken to make the four sounds evenly spaced. If, for instance, the ball of the left foot lands first, the ball of the right foot follows, then the left heel and finally the right heel. There must be the same interval between the right foot and the left heel that there is between the left foot and the right foot. When this doesn't happen the result is cramped indeed, and the roll is non-existent.

The second pattern is most useful in landing from bigger jumps such as tour jetés, cabrioles and air turns. Now the first foot lands and makes two sounds, ball-heel, followed by the second foot. These sounds also must be even and not kerplunk—pause—kerplunk.

There are many variations on these two themes. The first form may start with a slap followed by step, heel, heel. It may end with a stamp. It may start with a stamp on the right foot, for example, leaving the left foot in place and just using the heel of the left foot followed by step, heel on the right. Either form may be done in a continuous sequence. You can use the first form very effectively in brush, assemblé, cramp-roll in fifth, brush on the opposite side, assemblé, cramp-roll in fifth. In this combination the back foot always lands first, so don't practice them on your favorite side only. They are also valuable at the end of pull-backs and wing combinations.

In all variants, the important thing is to be sure that they are not "cramped" and that they do "roll." To achieve perfect control of the sounds in a cramp-roll takes a great deal more practice than you might imagine. A good plié is indispensable as it is in most steps. The results are well worth the effort, and the effort is, of course, worth more than anything.

Pull-backs

A pull-back is a tap made by the front part of the foot striking the floor while the body is in the air moving backwards. It is performed by standing on the ball of one foot, doing a plié, springing up and toward the rear, and lowering the jumping foot from the ankle till it makes audible contact with the floor, raising it again and finally landing on the ball of the foot with the leg in plié. It may also be done landing on the other foot from the one you begin on. The most difficult part of pull-backs is the start, with the weight on the ball of the foot and heel raised. If you begin with a flat foot on the floor you are forever stuck with having to make a flat-foot "clump" before you begin the step. This does not refer to beginning from a flat foot if the heel has been lowered separately, after the ball of the foot, to make two distinct sounds. For example: step, step, step, shuffle, pull-back (1 and 2 and 3 and 4)—the third "step" must be on the ball of the foot. Or: step, step, heel, shuffle, pull-back; not step, step, clump, shuffle, pull-back.

The pull-back is a very valuable asset in that it can be used to add a sound with very little physical movement and with very little change in the shape of an already chosen pattern. This makes possible the accomplishment of long running rhythms combined with long flowing movements (a sort of happy combination of Bill Robinson and Pavlova). It is also valuable in adding smoothness to the rapid-fire punctuations of trills and grace notes with which a tap dancer may choose to embellish certain parts of a dance. Remember that "backwards," in relation to pull-backs, refers to a line drawn through the toe and heel of the working foot, not just back from down-stage.

Wings

A wing is a quick flick of the foot to the side and a return to the starting position. As the foot returns it contacts the floor to make a tap before landing. This inward movement is in fact a slap to the side. There are three sounds in a wing. The initial sideways movement makes a scraping sound on the floor, the foot slides outwards, and the return of the foot makes two taps, as in a slap. The "scraping" is done with the outside of the front part of the winging foot. The inside of the foot must lift up slightly as the wing begins, in order to force a close contact between the outside edge of the shoe and tap with the surface of the floor. If you have rubber half-soles (recommended), it is advisable to cut the edges back about a quarter of an inch to make sure the shoe-to-floor contact produces a scrape instead of a brake. (See Chapter 4.)

This is a description of the technique of a wing. It's easier said than done. To begin with, it is performed with the weight on the winging foot. The other leg must be free to move in any desired pattern. In practice it is advisable to stand on both feet, with the weight on the non-winging foot, and just get used to the movement of the step. It must start with the foot pointed forward, or even a little inwards—very definitely not turned out. It requires a good plié to begin and to finish. It starts from the ball of the foot with the heel raised, and it lands in the same way. After having become familiar with it on both feet, you should practice dropping onto your heel in a controlled movement after landing on the ball of the foot. There are numerous ways of using the other leg: battements, développés in or out, ronds de jambes, and passés are some. Whatever movement you choose, you must be sure that the effort of the wing does not mar its execution. Heaving shoulders and flailing arms and jerking legs are an indication that you have not yet learned how to do wings.

Wings are of great value in adding sound to a large movement and sharp accents to a small one. They will also lend you
the appearance of being able to float over the stage. You will
feel as if you are floating. I dare to go a step further and tell
you that in fact you will float. Of course to do this you must
forget entirely about doing wings; follow the instructions of
Peter Pan and just "think lovely thoughts."

③ Turnout for tap dancers

Should one be turned out to tap dance? The answer is sometimes yes and sometimes no. This is a very unsatisfactory answer, and I shall attempt to explain it.

A tap dancer must remember that any kind of dancer must first of all be able to dance. The taps are, in my estimation, an added means of expression and communication, and seldom a source in themselves. So, as I have counseled before, a good basic training in movement of the body and limbs is essential. In much of this training a turnout is most necessary. Therefore, whenever a movement which you select stems from a basic turnout, you should be turned out no matter what form of tap step you may be doing. This would cover most ballet positions and some jazz movements. There are many jazz movements which demand a turn-in, and in these don't hesitate to turn in. This is all quite obvious as a general principle for large movements. It becomes more complex as we examine specific tap steps.

Slaps

Forward and backward slaps are done without turnout. The feet are parallel and close together. Slaps to either side are also done with no turnout. There are, however, many instances of slaps used as part of a larger movement. In a glissade, for example, beginning from fifth position, right foot in front, to do the step to the right side you will move the right leg to the right and close the left leg in back again in fifth position. If you use slaps in this movement, the right foot will make the first slap. It will be a forward slap so far as the foot is concerned, but it will be a turned-out leg and foot which make it. You will face front, and your toe will move in a line parallel to the line of the glissade. The left foot will follow, also turned out, to make a back slap and finish in the same fifth position from which you started. This principle is adhered to when you change feet in the glissade as well. Never try to do a glissade by using side slaps.

Many jumps in tap dancing use a slap-heel on one foot and a brush on the other as a preparation. For this, be as turned out as you would be in ballet. If you are facing front and wish to do a preparation for an assemblé or a jeté to the right, point the left foot to the left, well turned out, lead with the heel of the left foot, and do a back slap to fifth position in front of the right foot, lower the heel to the floor as you plié, and brush the right foot to the right side. Keep in mind that though this is a back slap, you are not moving backwards. Your line of movement is across the floor. In a similar preparation for a cabriole, which is a forward moving step, take care to start with a side slap forward in order to bring your heel as far to the front as you can before you take off.

Slaps are often used as a preparation for a wing. In this case you must turn the foot in to start the wing as you finish the forward slap. A wing always begins with a slightly turned-in foot so that you can scrape to the side, turn the foot out and return to the starting point with an inward slap before you land. In a series of wings with grands battements, the lifted leg is, of course, turned out as it rises in éffacé position. As it returns to the floor, it does a back slap and changes from being turned out to being turned in as you prepare for the next wing on the other foot. Follow the above carefully. It isn't as complex as it sounds, and it is the only way to produce the same smoothness of movement as, I trust, you now produce in sound.

Shuffles

In their simplest form, such as step shuffle, step shuffle, or as used in a waltz clog, shuffles are done with a moderate turnout.

The feet should point about forty-five degrees away from your center line. Less than this, and you will look cramped; more, and you're doing a sailor's hornpipe (no reason why you shouldn't if you mean to, but don't do it by accident). In hop shuffles you must be able to change at will from shuffling with the knee straight forward to shuffling with the leg turned out so as to bring the foot behind the supporting foot. It is valuable to practice hop shuffle knee to the front, hop shuffle knee to the side, to produce a 1 *and a* 2 rhythm. In this exercise the hip rotates ninety degrees out and in, and you should feel at ease in either position. Which you use depends on the step that follows—like fingering at the piano.

The shuffle to use before a pull-back is invariably turned out (eccentric steps might prove an exception). Not only turned out, but as far to the back as your plié and leg length will allow. Stand on your left leg with the foot facing forward, plié on the ball of the foot, stretch the right leg to the back as far as you can with the right foot just off the floor and turned out, as it would be in a low arabesque. Try to keep the hips level. Now shuffle with the right leg in this position, and pull back on the left. Either do or don't change feet for the landing, but try to finish in the same position from which you started. Nothing looks worse than shuffling forward as a preparation for a pull-back, so practice what I have outlined above. A forward shuffle also leaves you with a slightly backward orientation of your weight, which makes it more difficult to do the pull-back. Good pull-backs demand that the weight be over the supporting foot. The pull-back itself is done with the foot in exactly the line of travel of the step, and the shuffling or brushing foot is always turned out.

Take care not to let the hips swing from side to side. They should remain in a line at right angles to where you are facing. Swinging them around as you reach to the back for your shuffles is a weak substitute for not being turned out.

Cramp-rolls

In this step also there are times to be turned out and times not
to be. Let us consider first the cramp-roll which consists of
landing ball R, ball L, heel R, heel L. This is the most common
cramp-roll, and the one usually learned by beginners. If you use
it to land from a jump to the side with the feet together, then
land with the feet parallel, not turned out. This would apply to
most jazz movements and to any kind of a jump where the
knees remain together during the jump. If the knees are, the
feet should be, and you mustn't move them as you land. Hold
everything firmly together as you would in skiing a tempo turn
(non-skiers investigate). The secret of achieving four clear sounds
in a cramp-roll on landing from a jump is to point your toes till
they touch the floor.

Now, if you do a jump where the legs are separated at the
peak of the movement, such as an assemblé, then land in fifth
position with the feet turned out. Always keep as close as you
can to the fundamental shape of whatever step you do. You will
find it is no more difficult to do a cramp-roll in fifth position
than with the feet pointing forward. Changements are a very
good exercise to make you at ease with this form of cramp-roll.

If you land ball R, heel R, ball L, heel L, it usually indicates
that you are doing a step in which one foot lands well before
the other, and in which you have considerable momentum. In
this case be turned out, and adopt a fourth position as you land.
Your balance will be better, and your momentum will be more
easily arrested. An example is a landing from a cabriole or a
tour jeté. In the former you would arrive at a fourth position
forward; in the latter a fourth position to the back.

In general, you can figure out for yourself whether your step
should be turned out or turned in. Be sure you do figure it out
out beforehand and are certain of how you mean to do it. In-
decision is the most openly revealed characteristic a dancer can
have, and should be avoided like jingle taps.

4 Shoes and taps

Shoes

I have been asked many times to write about shoes and taps for tap dancers. I had always thought that the basic needs were self-evident and not worth detailed examination. But I have seen so many examples of bad shoes and bad taps that I have come to the conclusion I was wrong. The subject needs examination.

The most important thing about a dancing shoe is that you can dance in it. This means that you can plié, relevé, and point your foot very nearly as easily with your shoes on as without them. A shoe must be flexible in order to do this. Many are made of such stiff leather that it is very difficult to stand on the ball of the foot, and impossible to show a point. First, be sure that your shoe is made of pliable leather.

Some shoes have a shank that is too long and too stiff. A shank is a stiffening piece, usually made of metal or hard leather, about half an inch wide, that extends forward in the sole from the heel of the shoe. If it is too long it will hold the shoe flat no matter how you hold your foot. Its purpose, to the shoe-maker, is to help the shoe to keep its shape and also to enable him to use cheaper and less durable materials in the construction of the shoe. Make sure that the shoes you buy can be bent into a downward arch without great resistance. If you are having the shoes made for you, specify a short shank.

Shoes for girls pose special problems, since there are certain esthetic standards involved. It is very difficult to find a shoe for girls that is fit to dance in and yet does not look like a walking shoe for your maiden aunt. Shoes with high heels and no sides

may be used on stage, particularly if the management is paying
for them, but for studying and for practice they are not practical. The high heel makes relevés almost meaningless, since your
heel is already nearly as high as you can lift it; pliés are im-
paired, since you are forced into too far forward a position when
you bend your knees; the calf muscle gets very little exercise;
and the entire body is thrown out of alignment. It's bad enough
to suffer this for the duration of a number in a show; it is inex-
cusable to subject yourself to it while you are learning to dance.
So choose a low-heeled slipper-like shoe with side support and a
short vamp.

By low-heeled I mean not more than a half-inch. There are
such shoes, and what's more they can be "sexy."

The leather, particularly the sole, as with men's shoes, must
be flexible and of good quality; there must be support for the
ankle; the shank must be short; and the heel must be low. Take
care that in achieving support for the ankle you do not get up-
pers so high that they cut into the bone on the inside or outside
of the ankle joint, or the back of the shoe curved so that it cuts
into the back of the foot.

All leather stretches with use. Buy shoes with a snug fit over
as heavy socks or stockings as you ever plan to wear. For girls
who dance without stockings, I advise peds. There should always
be something between the shoe and the foot. Unabsorbed per-
spiration not only harms your feet, it also rots the shoe leather.
For performance I always wear a pair of light white wool socks
first and then a very thin sock to match whatever else I am
wearing. In this way I have avoided blisters and sore feet during
the last twenty years of pretty strenuous performing. During
classes and for practicing, I wear heavy white wool socks.

Good shoes are expensive, but cost considerably less than
feet. They can also make a great deal of difference in your
dancing.

Taps

There are many sorts of taps on the market. The majority of them are worthless. Some can actually harm your dancing.

The first requisite of a good tap is that it be firmly fixed to your shoe. Any looseness, jingle or rattle, whether on the front tap or the heel tap, is a great detriment to the production of clear tap sounds.

The second requisite is that it be as small and as light as possible in order to produce clean, audible sounds. There are taps which cover half of the front of the shoe and all of the heel. Shun them as you would the plague. They serve no useful purpose whatsoever. Your front tap should be made of a single piece of aluminum alloy shaped something like this:

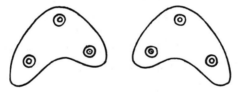

The heel tap should be made of a single piece of the same material as the front ones, and shaped like this:

There is no right and left for heel taps. There is for front taps, in order to have a slightly longer surface on the outside of each tap. This is to lend support to your foot as you bend it outwards for the initial movement of a wing. It also helps make the scraping sound that is part of the rhythm of the same step.

Both front and rear taps should fit exactly to the shape of the sole of the shoes—with the exception of the part of the tap you use for doing wings (the outside of each front tap, as just described). Here the tap should be *inside* the edge of the sole about an eighth of an inch. This is for two reasons. First, so that the edge of the tap will not catch on a splinter, a trap door, or an electrical outlet on the stage. Second, so that you can bend the foot on that side more easily as you begin a wing.

The taps should not protrude *beyond* the sole at any point, and any sharp edges should be rounded off with a file.

Now comes the most complicated part—the fastening of the taps to the shoes. The usual manner is to use nails or screws. This will serve for the heel tap, which is fastened to a rigid part of the shoe and has at least a half-inch thickness of leather for the nails, but not for the front taps. These invariably become loose, and the nails or screws either scratch up the floor or let the tap come off altogether. This is not very prevalent among beginners, but as soon as you start dancing more actively it inevitably happens. Repairs can be made by using wood inserts in the holes where the screws were, or sometimes by using larger screws. The taps will almost always come loose again, however. To my knowledge, there is only one sure way to fasten taps to shoes. This is to use rivets.

Riveting taps

Get some 5/8 inch or 7/8 inch flat-headed copper rivets with a shaft not more than 3/32 inch wide. Drill three holes through your taps with a drill of 3/32 inch width. Place the holes evenly, one in front and one on each side, about half an inch from the edge of the taps (see diagram). Countersink these holes with a countersink drill. Place the taps on your shoes exactly as they should be, the edges flush with the sole of the shoe except for the winging side. If some of the tap protrudes, leave it to be filed off after the tap has been riveted. Now, using a punch, mark the centers of the holes you have drilled on to the sole of the shoe. Remove the tap, take the sock linings out of the shoe (you can paste it back later), put the shoe on an iron last, and drill holes right through the sole with the same drill you used for the taps. Take the shoe off the last and insert the rivets from the inside of the shoe, so that the shafts protrude from the sole. This takes agile fingers and patience. When all three rivets are in place, put the shoe back on the last—be sure that the last is the right size, so that the flat heads of all three rivets rest on a solid surface. Fit the tap over the rivets and press it gently down till it rests firmly on the shoe. If the rivet shafts project more than an eighth of an inch over the taps, cut them off with wire cutters till they are at that height. Now take a light hammer, and with even blows hammer the rivets till they fill up the countersink hollows in the taps. Hold the shoe solidly on the last as you do this so that it doesn't slip or slide. The copper rivet will flatten out very quickly, and you can ensure its final holding by using a drill punch with a rounded end. Hold this against the already hammered out copper and give a final few clinching blows with the hammer. Run your hand inside the shoe to make sure the rivet heads are flush with the inside of the sole. If not, the rivets are not hammered firmly, and they must be.

As soon as all is smooth inside, replace the sock lining, and you are ready to file the taps. Do this first on the bottom to smooth out the protuberances made by the rivets. Then file the tap to make it smooth and to remove all sharp edges.

All of this takes more time than the store would to nail on your taps for you. It's worth it. I have never known a tap fastened in this way to come off under any circumstances. You may have to tighten them up a little after a few hours of hard use, because the leather will compress slightly and allow some play in the tap. This is easily done by hammering the rivets again with the shoes on the last. Taps fastened in this way won't become loose, won't scrape the floor, and won't come off.

If it all sounds too complicated, then at least do this: use longer nails than necessary, and be sure that they fold over inside the shoe and are hammered flush against the last. This won't prevent taps from coming off, but it will keep them on a little longer than usual.

When your taps are on, I suggest putting rubber soles on the part of the shoe not covered by the tap. This is not only to prevent slipping on fast floors, but also to make a level surface on the bottom of your shoe. A tap is at least an eighth of an inch thick, and with a thin sole this can be very clearly felt as a hard ridge when you dance. Be sure to level the edges of the rubber sole so they don't catch on the floor and so they don't hold you back in slides on the side of the shoe.

One last word of advice on buying shoes and taps. The very best shoes and taps are, of course, made to order. The principles I have discussed should be adhered to when you order shoes. But whether hand made or ready made, make sure of one thing: don't be misled by the salesman trying to sell you something because it is what "they" are using now. The amorphous "they" has furnished reason for more unreasonable purchases and acts than any agent I can think of. Find out who "they" are, or better still, go ask a professional dancer to let you see his shoes and taps. The only valid "they" is you, and your own experience. No shoe salesman is a substitute.

5 The value of silence

Most of what I've written about tap dancing has had to do with the sounds your feet make. Now I'd like to tell you about not making sounds.

Man's written thoughts have shown an appreciation of silence, from the West's description of it as "golden" to the Orient's subtler admonition that the mouth of a wise man eats rice.

"Silence" is a relative term. All percussive instruments, including tap dancers, spend more time in silence than they do making sounds. The time between taps in any succession of steps is generally greater than the time occupied by the taps. If this weren't so, the ear would find it difficult to hear the rhythm. You can distinguish taps as taps only when they are separated by silence. This sort of silence is an integral part of percussive rhythm. It happens involuntarily. The silence which concerns us here is a willed silence—in other words, the decision to stop tapping in the middle of a dance in order to produce a certain effect which shall be a part of the dance.

Let me introduce a seemingly irrelevant illustration. When you sit in a bathtub and the faucet drips a little to make its lovely random rhythms, and melody, too, listen carefully to how much silence there is. Sometimes the pauses between drops of an expected pattern become so long that the suspense is heightened out of all proportion to the accident of how well the washer fits the valve. This silence is not organized, as are the spaces between taps, and if you splash around a lot or have new plumbing you won't hear it at all. But if you do experience it, you will very quickly become aware of the great importance silence plays in rhythmic patterns.

Now let us examine the role of intended silence as it applies to tap dancing. Most tap dancers like to dance a continuing succession of sounds. An example is a time step and a break. This is usually a pattern of eighth notes with the accent on one for six bars, followed by a two-bar break of a very similar pattern. Most dances are like this, especially the allegedly advanced professional-type routines. Tap, tap, tap, tap!—hold a beat and tap again. There is a reason for this. It is that all of us, like nature, abhor a vacuum. We fear that if we aren't doing something every second we will lose someone's attention, that the audience will surely get up and walk out of the theatre unless they have an unceasing succession of sounds and movements to engage them. This is not so, but most dancers, consciously or unconsciously, are firmly convinced that it is.

This urge to fill an empty space is most natural, and before you can use silence in a dance you must learn to control it. When you can stop for any amount of time without anticipating your selected re-entry point, you can start considering how to use a pause in a dance.

A good beginning is to substitute silence for one of your breaks. Dance for six bars, hit the downbeat of the seventh bar, and hold your position till the downbeat of the next phrase. You will probably find that your "position" since it was originally part of a moving step, is not a very effective one. Experiment until you find one that is. It must lead into your next step as well as hold its own for the two-bar break.

Now consider a slightly more advanced application. Suppose that your dance and the music have been mounting in intensity until you just can't find a rhythm and a step to match what must happen next. Try not doing anything, and project the pent-up climax through a complete and sudden cessation of sound and movement. For this to be effective you must mean it with every muscle and nerve. Believe me, it is no less exhausting than a difficult step. Your energy must continue to pour out, but it can be even more effective than your fanciest *tour de force.*

Another valuable method of using silence is in a very relaxed dance—a soft-shoe number, for example. Start with two simple repeated rhythm steps of two measures each, stop for two measures instead of doing it a third time, and then fill in the remaining two measures. Or it might be a three-measure step, one bar of silence, a measure of dancing, a measure of silence, a measure of dancing, and a silent measure to complete the eight-bar phrase. In a relaxed dance you might profitably explore the use of arms and shoulders to continue the rhythm while your feet remain still and your body is in a pose. Silence is usually accompanied by motionlessness, and is more intense if it is, but there are some occasions when it is helpful to move in silence. This is not restricted to arms, head and torso. You can walk and do some steps silently by curling your toes up so that the tap doesn't touch the floor. You can't do this if you use any of the jingle or loose taps, but dancers don't use them—such things are strictly for the amateur birds.

One further avenue to explore is this. Don't always begin, after a silence, on the first downbeat of a measure. There is usually an expection of this, and it is often more interesting not to do the expected. Try remaining silent until the off-beat (need I say the "and"?) after the first count in the bar you select to resume dancing.

Make up different kinds of rhythmic stops for yourself. They can be used for added intensity, for climax, for anticlimax, for an element of surprise, for relaxing moments, and for fun. Explore and find out for yourself.

I am not an advocate of sweet carbonated drinks for dancers, but, at the risk of being misunderstood, I do advocate the pause that refreshes.

⑥ About performance

The most important part of any dance, provided you can do it at all, is your *intent toward* and *relationship with* the audience.

Very often a dancer becomes so involved in dancing that that becomes both the means and the end of his performance. But when this happens, he is relinquishing the responsibility he accepted when he decided to become a dancer. He is in fact allowing a certain vain gratification to take the place of difficult, conscious, and other-directed work. ("Other-directed" is the opposite of self-directed.)

What do we mean by intent toward an audience? It is what you want the audience to understand, know and feel after seeing you dance that they didn't understand, know and feel before seeing you dance. It is what you hope to add to the total of each individual in the theater by means of your performance. To make up a dance without an intent is a form of sentimentality which may be excused only in the very young. There are as many intents as there are dancers and dances. Their common denominator is a conscious wish to add something to the experience of another human being.

The intent most often used is an intent to amaze or astonish. This makes the least demand on dancer and audience and is perhaps the safest way to begin exploring the meaning of having an intent. The intent to amaze is a beginning; it is better than nothing.

As your own personality and experience develop, so will the compass of your intentions. It is not necessary to have a world-shaking idea. It is quite enough to want to make someone happier for having seen your dance, or wiser, or more able to cope with whatever problems they may have. On a very major scale,

consider the second theme of the last movement of the Brahms
First Symphony. If you haven't heard it, try to do so. I think
you will know exactly what it means to have something added
to yourself when you have listened to it. Go to a revival of any
early Chaplin movie, and see if you don't know more about the
frailties and triumphs of your fellow man than you did before.
This doesn't mean that every dance you do must be equated to
Brahms or Chaplin. It means that a dancer, or any artist, should
intend to make a difference of some value in the world around
him by virtue of the work he has created. The amount of the
difference is the scale by which we judge greatness.

Relationship with an audience

Your relationship with an audience is quite separate from your
intent toward it. Your intent is concerned with your choice of
subject. Your relationship is governed by how you present your
intent. This includes everything about your performance from
the moment you walk into the theater until you leave it. It even
begins a little before.

You should look at the theater from the outside, at least at
the entrance the audience uses. What sort of house is it? What
sort of lobby? Are the chairs hard or soft? Is the balcony high
or low? Examine everything you can that might have an effect
on the mood of the audience before the show begins. Examine
all the sight lines and consider where you must project what you
want to do. Try to find the focal point of the audience. When
you look at a face that interests you, you can usually find a
center to that particular face—a spot that seems to be the essence of the person. If this is lacking, the face is often said to
be vacuous or flat. A theater, from the stage, can be regarded in
exactly the same way. It has a personality of its own, and it is a
great help to the performer to search for it and discover it. You
aim the essence of your dancing at the focal point of the house,
and you determine the framework of your relationship with this
as a starting point.

Having done this, the next step is to know exactly who you are, and what part of yourself you wish to emphasize for the particular dance you are doing. You must know if you are a serious person or light-hearted or comical or satirical or dull or a combination of all these things. This, naturally, is not quite as simple as saying it, and it sometimes costs a great deal to find out. Do the best you can with the tools at your command. Then cleave to your answer unswervingly till a better one comes along. The first moment to activate your relationship with an audience is when the curtain rises.

If you can also find out something about the audience, you should do so. Is it a dance audience? Are you part of a show which has relatively little to do with dancing? Is it a benefit? A matinee? Is the audience assembled on a weekday or a Sunday? All these things constitute data from which you must draw conclusions. An electronic brain would be helpful, but more expensive than the average dancer can afford. Feed the data into your own brain and arrive at some decision about whether the audience will be happy or sad, elated or despondent, high or low. Relate this decision to your *intent* toward the audience, and then decide how you are going to walk out on that stage, or dance out, or be found on stage in a set pose.

Once the curtain is up you don't have another chance to *begin* whatever it is you are going to do. The initial contact cannot be recreated. You can develop your relationship, you can lead it along many different paths, but you can neither undo nor change that first magic moment.

At this initial meeting, the audience and the dancer will both form an opinion of each other, which will form a basis for whatever happens between the two of you from then on. Anyone who has ever been on stage knows that long before an audience expresses its feelings by applause, you, the performer, have an idea as to whether they are a "good" or a "bad" audience. I put those words in quotes because they have very special meanings to a performer, not at all like their real meanings. What is meant when a performer says the audience is "good" is that the audience likes him; if it doesn't, it is called "bad."

You may be liked by the audience for many reasons that aren't directly associated with your dancing. They may like the color of your hair, or your costume, or the way the music you dance to is being played. It is important to try to find out just what it may be, besides your performance, that excites an audience. You may also be disliked for similar reasons, and then it is even more important to find out what they are. The better you dance or sing or act, the less do relatively extraneous matters intrude, but no matter how fine an artist you are there will always exist an appraisal of you as a person apart from your performance.

Consider taking a bow, for example. Do you remain in the character of your dance? Do you become effusive in your humility or stern in your scorn? Just what do you feel when the dance is finished and a mark of momentary success or failure reaches your ears? And how do you express what you feel? I can point out the facts to be considered, but you must supply your own answers, and recognize how they affect you and your audiences.

Consider that no two performances are ever exactly the same. Not just technically, but in feeling as well. Some are up, some are down. What throws you into the mood of a wonderful performance? What makes you listless? Keep thinking about this until you have arrived at some sort of answer and then try to take advantage of what you find out. Don't be satisfied with "I don't know what it was—I just didn't feel right."

If an audience likes you and appears to be ready to accept anything you do, then make a special effort to be technically perfect. Dance as well as you possibly can, and resist the impulse to rest on the laurels of your personality. If they seem to dislike you, then concentrate on finding out why and showing a part of yourself that they will like.

Think about all these things, and be definitely conscious of your relationship to an audience.

There are those rare and wondrous instances in which your intent toward the audience, your relationship with them, and the dance you do are all so beautifully interwoven that there is no separation between them. In this case you will have gone through everything we have discussed, you will have nothing to worry about. You'll be dancing like an angel.

7 So you want to give a recital?

Someday you may want to do a tap dance recital. I've done hundreds, and can let you in on some of the tribulations that accompany the joys.

The first thing I usually need are some new dances. Some classical ones for a first group; a jazz dance and a satirical dance for later in the program.

Now, to find music which is playable by an accompanist and at the same time something that can be danced to. It must bear some relationship to your own life attitudes and fit with dances you already have. It would be nice if you could unearth some fine works by some little-known 17th- or 18th-century composer. You see yourself being hailed not only as a dancer, but also as a musical historian. Search, listen, haunt music stores, remember, think! You do this for two weeks and then settle on two well-known preludes by Bach.

You're also looking for a solid jazz piece. You even listen to juke-box tunes. They all have words which appear to have a considerable effect on most listeners, though you can't understand them yourself—especially some of the newest ones. You need something without words, or at least without vocal effects, because you want to make up your own idea for the dance. You decide to ask a good jazz-pianist to compose a work for you.

Now how do the shoes and costumes look? You need new ones. What sort? What color? Shoes are easy. The same man has been making them for you for many years. You order some. But the costumes? You start making the rounds of stores. You want a fancy waistcoat—not too fancy, just something that will have both style and color. You walk through every big fabric house in the city and most of the small ones. Salesmen envisage orders for curtaining and upholstering a ten-room apartment, and are remarkably calm when asked for a yard of you-weren't-quite-sure-what for a waistcoat you hadn't decided on.

Desperation speeds decision, and you soon have no less than five possible waistcoat backs and three fronts. Off to the tailor, who rejects them all as being impossible to make up into practical costumes. Out again with a blindfold and a prayer and a thinning wallet. You find, at last, what you're sure you wanted in the first place, and perhaps your wife can use what the tailor can't.

You've started to work on the two Bach preludes and have just emerged from those dreadful first hours during which your pianist plays the pieces and you stand in the middle of the bare rehearsal hall waiting for the walls to suggest an opening step. You now have the opening step and are standing motionless waiting for the walls to suggest a second step. Space never looks so empty as it does before you fill it.

The hall has been engaged, and you are reminded of it when your manager calls and asks what sort of folder you want to send out and to whom you want it sent. You're sure that this part of giving a recital somehow takes care of itself, but it doesn't. It means a trip to the printer, who always has his shop in one of the less accessible areas of the city. You bring along some photos, some line drawings, and some very rough ideas of how to describe yourself and your program—or shall you use quotes from reviews? But there aren't any quotes for unperformed dances. You'll work it out.

You arrive at the large downtown building that houses the printer. You've ridden your bicycle. The man won't let you in with it, and you've forgotten your lock. You assume the role of a bicycle advertising agent, and tell the man you have to have it photographed at the printing shop. He eyes you suspiciously, and grudgingly takes you up in the freight elevator.

The man who's going to print the three thousand folders is

very helpful, and asks what you want on the folder. "What size print and what color stock would you like?"

Gradually ignorance lessens and confusion grows. You become conversant with the world of the printer. Shiny stock, dull stock, colored stock, bold face, light face, wide face, narrow face, and your own becomes increasingly red. From all this one has to select words and empty space to make some sense on a foldable sheet of paper.

Back to the tailor's, where you discover the pants are too long and you have entirely forgotten the costume for the jazz number. This tailor can't make them in time, so you hunt for another. You reopen the search for material, this time for jazz pants and a wild shirt. The pants are relatively simple. The shirt leads you to every department store in New York. You finally find one that is perfect, but it has short sleeves and you need long ones. You buy two shirts and think to make two long sleeves from the extra shirt. Unimaginable how much cloth and sewing goes into a shirt sleeve! It can be done, but it costs more than both shirts together. Short sleeves from now on.

Now for taps on the shoes. This is, from long practice, quite easy. What isn't counted on is the fact that on a very fine stage, such as exists at the 92nd Street YMHA, the least difference in the sound of your right and left taps shows up very distinctly. To make them sound alike is a process of arduous hand filing. Make the heavier one thinner and find the high spots. Try them on again. File some more. Finally they are sufficiently close to be acceptable. The jazz shoes aren't ready yet because they have to be dyed to match the jazz pants. Calf skin won't dye, so they've used goat skin. The shoes are ready the day before the concert—they look lovely. You rush to break them in by going through the dance a few times. After sliding around a little, you discover that the goat skin, being softer than calf, has stretched to such an extent that you have to wear two pairs of socks to feel comfortable.

The night before the concert the costumes arrive. Try them on. Splendid. Wait a minute! The pants are now too short. The concert is tomorrow, Saturday. Lights aren't set yet. Final rehearsal with lights, drummer, and pianist is set for 12 noon Saturday for the 8:30 curtain. A small kingdom for a Saturday tailor!

A magician is found who not only lengthens the pants but fixes a waistline and a waistcoat button. The jazz shoes are touched up with a daughter's paint box, and you get to the theater at 12:45, ready to rehearse. You hang up your clothes, open the suit case and discover your make-up box isn't there. You were sure you had remembered everything, but no amount of searching unearths the make-up box. Nothing to do but go home and get it.

As you leave the stage, the crew asks about your lights. You have outlined them, but they have to be set and tried and focused, which can't be done without you. You're back soon, though, and the light rehearsal begins.

The crew of two at the YMHA is very skillful, and everything moves along. But no matter how skillful people are, there is always a considerable difference between what you imagined and what they produce. How dark is dark blue? And how light is light straw? You would like more front lighting, but there isn't any. This means you spot for turns on an exit light—and there are five of them to look at. Also, since there aren't any footlights, the absence of front lighting means that the whole downstage area is very dim, and you wonder how clearly you will see the front edge of the stage during a flying circular step. The stage manager suggests that a strip of white adhesive tape could be laid along the edge of the stage as a guide line. You agree. Ordinarily you prefer not having footlights, since it means the audience can see your feet better, or rather that you can show them off better. But seldom do you find a stage without both foot and front lights.

As you are musing on this point, your accompanist arrives and you discover it's a little after four, and you should be ready to go through some dances. But you're not half finished with the lighting. So you press him into service as a stand-in for you while you sit out in the orchestra to see how the lights look. Your accompanist is a handsome man, and he looks fine. You wonder if you could show him all your dances and have him do the show for you. Alas! You never learned to play the piano.

The last filing for equal tone of the taps on your shoes has left them a little rough, so you start smoothing them out by doing about a thousand slaps while you call out suggestions for lights and mark a program for curtain cues. You are ready to go through your first dance when a totally strange man appears out of the wings and says he's come to see someone about the sheaves—yes, the "sheaves." Bewildered, you call the stage manager and he engages the man in what turns out to be a mutually satisfactory discussion. You never find out what "sheaves" are.

Now the jazz dance begins with the drum as the curtain rises, and though you can always give the right tempo when you are rehearsing, you can hardly expect to count off a solid beat with a listening audience. It takes more tries than you would think for all three of us—pianist, drummer and dancer—to arrive out of very thin air at a tempo that satisfies us all. We do arrive at one, and all of us pray we can recapture it at about 9:45 that night.

This dance finished, you return to the classical opening numbers, and are just discovering you haven't as much room as you had in rehearsal hall and will have to change the opening step when the box-office manager apologetically interrupts.

"Mrs. M. is on the phone and says you promised her four seats. We don't seem to have them. What shall I tell her?"

Indeed you had promised her four seats, and had just plain forgotten them. By this time all your free house seats are gone. Nothing to do but buy them.

You've worked out the lights for the Sonata, the dance without music, but you haven't danced it for several days because of emphasis on the new numbers. Here goes. Accompanists can have a cup of coffee, or dinner even.

Just as you start the first movement the piano tuner arrives. You remember he is supposed to come, but you hadn't realized it was so late. There isn't any other time he can do it, so you dance a sixteen-minute unaccompanied dance to the strange but necessary chromatic sequences and octaves that only a piano tuner can produce. He never looks up, even at your best steps.

How about your own food? It's too late to have a meal, but you should eat something. There's a restaurant across the street from the YMHA. You order a steak, bread and butter, and a glass of milk. You eat four mouthfuls of the steak. That's enough. Not for the waiter it isn't: "Something wrong with the steak?" "No, it's fine. I have to dance later, so I can't eat much." "Whaddya mean you have to dance?" "I just mean I have to give a show, a dancing show, that's all." "It's a compulsion or something?" I finally explain to his satisfaction and leave with the disturbing thought that it probably is a compulsion.

Back to the theater. Half an hour's rest. Well, twenty minutes anyhow. You begin to put make-up on at about 7:15. Curtain is 8:40. Make sure you have enough time to warm up well. Sometimes you skimp because the excited feeling before a show makes you feel as if you were warmed up. You know better. On stage to limber at eight o'clock. The curtain is down. Piano must be exactly placed. You must have room for the drummer, for your own exits and entrances.

Final light check and stage check. Looks good. Sounds good. You hear a strange voice from the audience side of the curtain. People! Somebody will be there because you're going to dance. That hidden fear of an empty house vanishes. It's immediately replaced by the fear of a full house. The more to witness your mistakes and slips.

Just a few more grands battements. You're slightly moist and well warmed. Back to the dressing room. Opening costume to put on. It feels strange, but it fits. Some of your students have found their way backstage and stand looking at you with glowing silence. Can they do something for you? Everything moves, and so do they.

"Show time, Mr. Draper."

You walk on stage. The volume of sound on the other side of the curtain is considerable. It's 8:40. The stage manager says to give them five minutes. Pianist is seated and smiling. A blessing.

Another thirty seconds to collect yourself. Stand up. Legs be strong, feet be light. House lights start to dim out. Voices are stilled. Curtain!

You walk on stage. There is a reception, and you acknowledge it. It seems to be very generous. You hope your dances are as well received as you are. Friendly, friendly, warm and nice. It stops. There is a huge silence. You look around. No, there's nobody else on stage but you. Can't find anybody anywhere. You'd better do something. You'd better dance your heart out. Now.

⑧ At ease

One of the most attractive features about any form of dancing is the ease with which it appears to be done. "Effortless" is a key word in praising a dancer. This doesn't imply that the dancer sits in a rocking chair; it means that the energy used in the dance is not obviously apparent. Tap dancing has often been a lone exception to this particular criterion.

In fact, praise is sometimes given to tap dancers in inverse proportion to the effortlessness of their work. Phrases such as "beating his brains out," "tearing up the stage," and "laying down a lot of iron," are used to indicate admiration rather than criticism. Of course this isn't so about the very greats, like a ~~Bill~~ Brian Robinson or a Fred Astaire; they are always discussed in the same terms that are used for any other kind of dancer. As one descends the scale it appears that virtues are made of inadequacies. Since so many people learn a little tap dancing and since a little tap dancing is almost invariably dreadful, it is sounder to consider what happens as praiseworthy rather than to try to change what happens.

Now it isn't too difficult to make tap dancing a fit subject for the same sort of criticism that is applied to other forms of dancing. There are very few steps in tap where apparent effort cannot be replaced by apparent ease. Exceptions are such steps as the one which starts standing on the balls of both feet with the feet parallel and close together, then jump off the floor, brush out left, brush out right, brush in left, brush in right, land left, land right, lower left heel, lower right heel. This makes eight fast sounds to one quarter note of a medium four. I have yet to be able to do it without making it look almost as hard as it is. There are some others which I will be glad to write out for anybody who wants them, but by far the majority of tap steps that are usually done *in extremis* and with monstrous labor can really be done with such apparent ease that they never interfere with the overall pattern of the dance.

What is apparent ease, and why does one dancer look so much more relaxed than another while performing the same step? The work is performed is equal to the mass times the velocity, and it has to be performed, or the step, whatever it may be, just doesn't get done. If you lift a leg, you lift a leg and if you don't you don't. The real effort involved must be exactly the same. Only the audience thinks it isn't. To the audience one dancer moves easily, another doesn't. There are many reasons for this. Some of them you can do something about, and some you can't.

Innate skills are beyond your control. In this area you are either a have or a have-not. The quality of muscle response and its adaptation to training is to some extent a matter of luck, good or bad. If your luck is bad, then realize it as early as you can and find some other form of expression. Otherwise you will beat your brains out and get nothing for your pains as well. If, however, you have enough innate skills to be able to successfully coordinate the several movements of a wing with a grand battement and keep time while you do it, then there is a good chance for you to achieve as much effortlessness and ease as you would like within, say, six months of beginning to learn it.

One of the more obvious questions is, of course, how hard are you prepared to work to learn any particular step. If you will practice a wing, for instance, a hundred times a day correctly on each foot for three months it's more than likely you'll do wings more easily than you did before. They may not be quite what you want, but they'll certainly be better than average, because "average" never really practices at all after learning.

By far the greatest aid to apparently easy tap dancing is not directly concerned with how hard you concentrate on a specific step. It has to do with your ability to isolate the muscles that are involved in doing the step from those that aren't. This is a difficult process, but one of great value. It is the secret of apparent effortlessness.

Examine the exact movement requirements of a pull-back or a shuffle or a wing. Feel out for yourself or ask your teacher what muscles are essential for that particular movement. Then try to do it without using any other muscles. This means not only physical awareness of a high order, but also a psychological awareness. A large number of movements one makes are responses to fear, insecurity, or socially unrewarding behavior. In other words, if you have a fear that you may not succeed in doing a certain step, and if you are used to being punished for failure, then it may easily happen that you will bring into play certain muscle groups unrelated to the step but necessary for defense.

There are, of course, many contributing factors in this situation. Everyone desires to be accepted. The need for this is often the primary motivation for deciding to become a dancer and go on the stage. Equally, most of us have a distaste for not being accepted. It is the threat or fact of non-acceptance that leads to many of the involuntary movements of defense, causing a dancer to appear ill at ease.

If a pattern of non-acceptance in one's non-dancing life has included physical punishment, then it is natural to raise a shoulder to ward off a remembered blow, or threat, at a time when one is in a situation that might lead to non-acceptance as a dancer. This doesn't mean that you think the teacher or the audience is actually going to hit you if you miss a tap. It is just that the fear of failure to succeed may easily stimulate your subconscious to make you act as you did in other situations when you were punished for failure, or scolded, or made to feel ostracized.

Non-acceptance is a delicate matter. A look can be just as effective as physical punishment in building patterns that lead to disturbing gestures. A desire for acceptance leads to movements of aggression as well as defense. A need to protest against a real or imagined order of things has caused many a foot to slip and ligament to tear. It is not the purpose of this chapter to attempt an analysis of all the matters outside the technical realm of dancing that may engender harmful or unrewarding physical movements, but I think it can be said that a desire to maintain one's sense of identity has invented as many steps as Bill Robinson.

Let us examine some of the more obvious habits that are definitely not caused by any physical malfunction or lack of knowledge, but that impair the desirable "at easeness" of a dancer.

Looking at your feet or the floor

The reason usually given for the head down position is that it helps to do the step since you can watch your feet. This is palpably ridiculous. By the time you have detected a false move it is already completed and your eye will in fact look for a balance or symmetry that can only be found by repeating the same mistake.

It is much more likely that the real reason is a desire to hide yourself ostrich-like, from the audience or the teacher, to avoid being identified by face as the one who made the mistake you anticipate making. You can learn to hold your head up and look out either by being sure you're not going to make a mistake or, far better, realizing that there is no law saying you have to be perfect. So you make a mistake—so what? The world will not end. Nor will you.

If neither of these remedies work, my advice is to wear a mask. No one ever lived who was unable to look any audience in the eye from behind a mask. They are hot and expensive, but they'll do the job.

Hands like fists and arms held in

The description of this movement pattern is its own explanation. It is a traditional pose of both defense and attack. It looks not unlike a boxer, and is more often adopted by men than by women. It is one of the worst looking of the not-at-ease symptoms. It is explained by the dancer either in terms of not being able to coordinate arms and legs or by having concentrated too hard on the feet.

The real reason is that fear of failure or criticism has resulted in a pose that will protect against attack, and in fact enable one to ward off a critic not just be defense but by counterattack. You hit me and you'll be hit back. No such thought could be further from the dancer's mind, yet I'm sure that in the cool aftermath of a hot performance some dancers have contemplated a bodily attack on an unresponsive audience. I guess if you could step down from the stage and actually hit some individual embodiment of your frustration it might enable you to use your arms and hands more freely forever after.

Since that avenue is impractical it remains to develop a sureness within yourself that renders you impregnable. Your love and skill can be an armor stronger than any of the knights wore. It is possible to hold your arms out or in because the dance asks it and because you can withstand any attack made on you. Your hands no longer clench to semi-fists or rigid paddles because you don't need to hit anyone. You're at ease. Your strength is in the dance and in you.

Believe me, it isn't that simple but it can be done.

⑨ A place to lay your feet

Dancing began with the ground as a stage. You danced wherever you were when you wanted to dance. If the ground was hard or pebbly you acquired tough feet.

In many countries the earth is still used as a dancing floor. In fact, until recently it was considered a treat to beat your feet on the soothing mud of Mississippi. However, most dancing to-day is done on a prepared surface called a stage. It is usually made of wood, though sometimes of stone or concrete. Depend-ing on its main use, it has a surface of wood, cloth or linoleum.

Tap dancers and Spanish dancers are especially sensitive about the surface they dance on because it affects the quality of the sounds they make when they dance. Whereas a ballet company needs a ground cloth on many stages and is able to feel secure on it, a tap dancer does not. He wants to achieve a dry sound of medium pitch without reverberation. He also needs a surface that is smooth without being slippery. If the theater is on the small side and has good acoustics, a heavy linoleum covering on a well-constructed wooden stage is ideal. There aren't many such in my experience, and I will settle for a hard maple stage, which is also hard to find.

Since I have given performances in several hundred cities in this country and abroad, in both theaters and night clubs, I have had considerable experience in trying to find an ideal place to lay my feet. I began to learn to tap on what is called a dancing mat. I think these no longer exist, so a word of explanation is in order. They were made of thin strips of hard maple about an inch wide and perhaps eight or ten feet long. These were glued

55

or riveted to a very heavy canvas backing, side-by-side, in sufficient number to make whatever reasonable width one wished.
Some were eighteen feet or so long. By turning them upside
down you could roll them up and have a relatively small but
heavy package. I never used one on stage, but many dancers did.
The sound was lovely, but the space was limited, and transporta-
tion difficult.

The first floor I used on stage was marble. It was circular—
two feet in diameter and about an inch and a half thick. It was
mounted on a pedestal two feet high with a very heavy base so
it wouldn't rock. It made a sharp, light sound, and very nearly
prevented me from ever learning to dance at all. I became famous, in a very small way, as a "flash act." One fast number,
on and off, and that was it. I finally broke it up one night at a
Los Angeles vaudeville house.

My next booking was at the Chicago Theater. It was May
Day week, and the producer had thoughtfully arranged a number in which, standing on the pedestal, I was to end my dance
holding a towering maypole. The girls in the chorus were each
to hold one of the ribbon streamers hanging from the pole and
dance around until the pole and I, plus pedestal and they, were
inextricably bound together. It was an appealing idea, but it de-
pended on the pedestal, and there was no pedestal. The theater
lawyer searched the contract in vain, there was no clause that
stated I had to dance on a pedestal. As a result I danced on the
stage itself that week and for the first time discovered the joys
of what appeared to be unlimited space. It took several years
for me to learn to make use of it.

Stage floors, however, I found, were very dissimilar. Some
made a good sound, and some were dreadful. And though there
wasn't much one could do about it in movie theaters and night
clubs, one could control it to some extent in concert halls. This
was so because concert halls were vacant much of the time and a
floor surfacing could be laid before the performance.

With this knowledge I had made for me a mammoth portable
floor. It was in six-foot-square sections. Each section was made
of fine oak panelling. It was designed and constructed by Sloanes,

and cost $2,500. It cost very nearly that much to ship it to
New Haven for its first use. I was up most of the night disas-
sembling it and arranging for its packing and freighting. Just as
it was about to be taken to the station to be forwarded to Den-
ver I had an inspired thought. I ordered it shipped back to
Sloanes. I never saw it again and learned much later that it
graced the hall, library and dining room of a large mansion.

There had to be a simpler way. There was. Plywood and
masonite were just becoming popular. They were both light and
hard surfaced. I tried some in a lumber mill. The sound was
fine. It could be ordered in each city at a nominal cost, nailed
over the existing floor, and every problem would be solved.
Little did I forsee the new problems that would be created.

The problem of stage floors was a continuing one in the days
of my early tours. No matter how careful the wording in a contract as to what constitutes a slippery or a rough stage, there
was always the subjective element, which was unpredictable. For
instance, the chairwoman of the concert committee in Cloven
Hoof, Idaho, had a very definite idea about slipperiness. Her
waxed linoleum hallway was slippery. The stage floor was not
covered with waxed linoleum, therefore it wasn't slippery. Or a
gentleman in Rubber Boot, Montana, had a barn floor that he
knew was rough. The auditorium was no barn and therefore
it wasn't rough. This may be a slight exaggeration, but only
slight. So, getting panels of plywood or masonite secured to
each stage floor seemed to be the solution.

Plywood seldom varied if you ordered the same thickness
and grade, and that was fine. But, plywood wasn't always avail-
able, and masonite usually was. The masonite I had tried out
was perfect. Sound and surface were ideal. So, where there
wasn't any plywood, I ordered masonite. But some of it proved
to be slick as ice and some of it rough enough to afford sure
ascent up a wall. It isn't labeled in any way I could fathom and
I never knew until the afternoon of the concert whether I was
going to slide or stick.

There was a memorable day in Kansas City. The auditorium
was deep, and usually housed either symphony orchestras or

wrestling matches. The stage was impossible and masonite had been ordered. It had arrived but nothing at all had been done about sealing it down. It had to be nailed or it would slip around and leave gaps between sections. It was about 5:00 in the afternoon. The concert was at 8:30. I had been at Thomas Benton's house admiring some of his magnificent paintings and he had driven me to the auditorium. Larry Adler was with us when we all walked on stage together. Not only was it clear that we would have to do the work ourselves (the stage hands wouldn't be back until 7:30), but also it was apparent that the stage was filled with hollows and bumps. This meant that we had to nail every few inches or there would be hollow spaces under the masonite that would sound like a drum and act like a miniature trampoline. Thomas Hart Benton stripped off his coat, found a hammer, and set to work. The three of us laid the masonite floor in about an hour-and-a-half. I put my tap shoes on and discovered that this particular masonite was of the very slickest sort. I could barely stand up on it, let alone dance. We found sandpaper and, believe it or not, we sanded that stage by hand until minutes before curtain time. I then sprinkled it with powdered rosin, put on a quick make-up, and we started what turned out to be a very successful show. I was already warmed up. Hunger pangs set in about halfway through the evening, but my footing was secure. Mr. Benton is honored as a painter. Few know of his other talents.

Another memorable occasion was at the San Francisco Opera House. We naturally presumed that the stage of the opera house must be perfect. Hadn't they been giving operas on it for thirty years? Certainly a tap dancer and a harmonica player couldn't complain.

It was Sunday afternoon. Rehearsal was 11:00 A.M. and the concert was scheduled for 2:30. Lo and behold, the entire stage proved to be laid in small sections about two feet by three feet with cracks in between, so that no dancer could have danced on it. Plywood would have been fine on top of it, but on a Sunday afternoon there was no lumber yard open. Eventually it was discovered that the husband of one of the women on the committee

owned a lumber yard. He was prevailed upon to find a truck
and send a man to get the plywood. It arrived about 2:00. I began to nail it down. A voice rang out from the wings, "Hey! No
nails in this stage."

"What?" I said, "no nails in the stage?"

It was almost 2:15. The curtain was down, but the 3500
seat auditorium was nearly full.

After fervent pleas, it was allowed that I use nails on the
back part of the stage, but none on the apron. Since the apron
comprised almost half of the stage and was essential to performance, I asked that the curtain be raised. I explained the problem to the audience and, courtesy of their kind patience, I spent
the next twenty minutes fastening 4 × 8 sections of plywood to
the apron with adhesive tape, and I made a running commentary
as I worked and tried to warm up as I measured off the tape. It
turned out to be a very successful show. But no hand equalled
the one I received as the last section of plywood was finally
down.

I have written of some of the floors which had to be laid
down over existing stages. But there were times when the management insisted that no floor problem existed.

I remember with vivid clarity just such a situation in a
medium-sized town in the Midwest. We arrived the afternoon of
the concert and I hastened to the theater, put my tap shoes on
and felt out the stage. It was like a skating rink. The person in
charge of both theater and concert was a lady of forbidding
mien and unswerving determination. The stage was not slippery,
she pointed out, because it had no wax on it. The contract said
no wax and there was no wax. I showed her that I could slide
for several feet with a slight push. No, the stage was not slippery
because it had no wax on it. I never did find out what was on
it, but it set a new record for low coefficient of friction. No
appeals on my part were of any avail and the best I could do to
remedy the situation was to wet mop the stage. I sprinkled
some resin on it but the surface was impenetrable and the resin
just slid around. Show time arrived and I had practiced enough
so that I thought I could handle my dances without disaster. It

was simply a matter of taking off and landing without any pressure sideways—just push straight up and land straight down.

The lady in charge was an ardent knitter as well as theater manager and impresario. She didn't much care for dancing or anything theatrical. But she did feel a certain obligation to be on hand during the performance. So she sat in the wings with her back toward the stage and knitted. She chose this position not so much to avoid looking at the show, but rather so that the lights from the stage might fall over her left shoulder and illuminate her needles as they wove an intricate pattern.

She settled into this position some minutes before show time so that as the curtain rose she was well established on the opposite side of the stage from my entrance. My opening dance was to a Handel *Allegro*. It began off stage with a rushing run and the first step was a cabriole, right leg up, right arm raised, and a look of splendid confidence on my face. The landing was to be step heel, step heel to make four sounds (a cramp-roll). But I was literally sitting on air before coming down. It was an effective entrance and I had always enjoyed it. This time I got a good start and in my enthusiasm neglected to jump straight up. I tried for a little distance as well. As I took off, my left foot went completely out from under me. I got the elevation all right but without any balance or control, and I realized while I was in the air what was inevitably going to happen. It did. I landed in exactly the same position I held in the air. Sitting! It happened so neatly that the audience thought I always entered that way and was a great comedian. Since I was rendered immobile by shock and pain, I adhered to the vaudeville adage, "Stay down for your laugh." I stayed down long enough for the laugh and the pain to subside and on rising I explained humbly that the fall was not part of my act and that I would have to leave the stage for a few minutes to recover. As I turned to walk off, there was Madame, still seated, still not looking at the stage. She hadn't missed a stitch. I limped past her and she had the grace to look up. She immediately lowered her gaze and said in a loud, clear voice, "I see you made a faulty step." I have not forgotten those words. And I have tried diligently since not to make a similar faulty step.

10 What is rhythm?

Rhythm in tap dancing is the pattern of percussive sounds made by the feet within the framework of the accompanying music. The musical framework is defined by the meter, the beat, the melody and the rhythm of the music. The meter defines the duration and shape of the bar; the beat maintains the regularity of that shape; the melody is the horizontal succession of tones; and the rhythm of the music is the accent and time duration of those tones.

This may not seem to bear much relation to tap dancing, but unless you are tap dancing without music, any tap sounds you make will be a rhythmic addition to the already existing rhythm of the music you dance to. Even in tacit breaks there is an understood continuation of the music which must be taken into consideration when you make up your "breaks." So it is valuable to discuss rhythm in music in order to understand it in tap dancing.

In music, rhythm makes time intelligible. Human beings have a tendency to space accents evenly, because of the regularity of the heart beat and walking gait. Rhythm is also apparent in our speech. The need for communication of idea and feeling beyond the meaning of words made accent and pause essential parts of speech. There was also the influence of natural phenomena—the seasons, the sun, the moon and the stars. Rhythm, with sources inside and outside of us, is essential to us.

As melody developed historically it acquired an increasingly complex structure of rhythmic invention. Some of the first examples we have of ordered oral rhythm in art form are found in Gregorian chants. For the last three hundred years, much use has been made of poly-rhythms—one or more rhythms being played simultaneously. These may be expressed by counter melodies in different rhythms, or by having a rhythm section that not only plays the beat but also a distinct rhythmic pattern (as in the Bolero). Modern jazz has developed this branch of rhythm to a most complicated level.

Now we return to the rhythm a tap dancer makes. It is a special sort, since it can be only percussive and not melodic. A tap is not a sustained sound. Its patterns must be made up from a succession of short sounds of equal length and pauses of any length. It must be heard to be effective, and it must make sense beyond just keeping time. The origin of Lancashire clog dancing has been described as being due to the rapid consonant sound of the English language plus the innate desire of the Anglo-Saxon races to create difficulties for themselves. This may be true, but it doesn't serve as a model for a creative art. A tap dancer's sounds must make a conscious contribution to the overall effect of the dance. Just as you choreograph your stage movements and your steps to communicate a certain aspect of yourself and your relation to the world around you, so must you create your rhythmic structure.

Many tap steps just "keep time" and many more are done with whatever accents the physical exigencies of the step itself create. Take the well-known time step as an example: 4 and 1 and 2 and 3 and 4, etc. Its rhythmic pattern is a sequence of eighth notes with an accent on 1. This is not necessarily bad, but it isn't of much interest as a composition in percussion. It does mark time, which has a certain value, though to do it really accurately requires far more practice than it's worth. If you decide a sequence of eighth notes is necessary to your dance, you can certainly think up more interesting ways of doing it than shuffle-hop, slap, slap, step. (Incidentally, a variation of the time step is to make the rhythm a dotted eighth and a sixteenth in sequence. This also improves the look of the step.)

The best way to approach rhythm in tap dancing is to have the whole composition in mind. Ask yourself what the dance is about. Is it a delicate soft shoe? A fast jig? A wild jazz number? Think of the whole dance and build your rhythms along

with your steps. If you can't make the sounds you want with a
certain step, then use another step. Rhythm doesn't have to
match each bar, it can overlap and reach home at the end of
four, five, six or sixty bars. It can match the beat or be off the
beat. It is the architecture of the dance you dance. Above all it
must be firmly within the foundations that are built by the beat.
The beat lies inside of you, the rhythm you make is on the outside, and shows that you really know what you are doing.

Most beginners are led to believe that for each quarter note
you can make one, two, three or four tap sounds, or no sound
at all. This is very misleading. The number of tap sounds you
make for each quarter note is not arbitrarily fixed. It depends
on the time duration of the quarter note and how fast you can
dance. A good tap dancer should be able to make about twelve
taps a second, and at a slow tempo a quarter note lasts a little
more than a second. This means that sixteen taps to the quarter
note (sixty-fourth notes, not uncommon in music) should be
within the reach of a tap dancer.

Keep in mind that the number of taps to each count is not a
function of the quarter note. It is a function of your ability and
the tempo of the dance.

The notation of rhythmic patterns for tap dancers

The much-used 1 and 2 and 3 and 4 is both vague and limited.
It is vague because there is no indication of the position or value
of "and" and it is limited because it can be used justifiably only
to define a series of eighth notes. It is, in fact, used in many
other ways to the detriment of a dancer's understanding and
scope. For instance, slaps are often counted out as and 1 and 2
and 3, etc. Now slaps can be done in this rhythm but by far the
more usual way is in the form of a sixteenth note and a dotted
eighth (since taps have no lasting sonority it would be more
exact to write two sixteenths followed by an eighth rest—the result would be the same). You can get around this difficulty by
explaining that in tap dancing you indicate sixteenth notes by 1

uh and uh 2 uh and uh etc., or some similar guttural or aspirant exclamation. Then you can show the sound of slaps by uh 1 uh 2 and so forth. This leads, for indicating really fast steps, to some sixty uhs to the bar. This must be an Indian war dance or "Pass the Peace Pipe, Harold!"

We might be spared this approach through learning to divide time by the accepted musical method. It is no more difficult to learn than grunting. If anyone has any other ideas, I welcome them.

Now to some suggestions for rhythmic patterns.

Fast dances

This includes those dances, with or without music, which have a tempo of from sixty to eighty bars a minute. The rhythms most generally used are a sequence of eighth notes—two eighths and a quarter, or three eighths (in triplet form) and a quarter. The accent comes on the strong beats, 1 and 3. At this speed there is not much else you can do if your rhythms are limited to a series of single steps. Try thinking in longer rhythmic phrases than single steps allow. Take an eight-bar phrase and step on the first count of each bar in 4/4 time for five bars, then step on 1 and 3 of the sixth bar, 3 of the seventh bar and on 1 of the eighth bar. Like this: 1, 1, 1, 1, 1, 1, 3, 3, 1. It's a basic rhythm. Now do the whole eight-bar phrase in eighth notes and keep the same accents. Or just use the pattern of the last four bars, the 1, 1, 3, 3, 1 and repeat it. The eighth notes by themselves would lend only speed, but the underlying accents will add a very distinctive character.

Now step off two bars (ball changes will do) using one step to each count; 1 2 3 4, 1 2 3 4. Don't accent any beat. Then with large movements step two bars in three beats to the bar. Accenting each step. This is written as three half notes to the bar, with a line and figure three over them (triplets). If this sounds difficult think of each bar as one count, a whole note, and divide that one count into three parts. This will make three against four and, especially following the two bars of four steps each, it makes a very exciting rhythm at these speeds. The four bars counted out look like this: 1 2 3 4, 1 2 3 4, 1 2 3, 1 2 3. Naturally all the bars are the same length. It is only your division of them that changes.

Next try tapping out (ball changes again) this four-bar rhythm: 1 3 4, 2 3, 1 2 4, 1 3, Accent 1, 3, 2, 1, 4, 3, and repeat. This is more difficult than is apparent, but well worth working for. Naturally, the counts omitted are silent. When you can do this easily at speed with ball changes, add some of the steps that fit the two eighths and one quarter pattern, or the three eighths (triplets) and one quarter. These might be wings or pull-backs. A combination might be made up of step, wing, step, wing, step, pull-back (four sounds), step, step, wing, step, wing, step, pull-back, step. Be sure to retain the accents I have given.

These rhythms are just a few of the many possible ones. How you put them together and how long you use each one in a dance should be up to you. Your selection will depend not only on your skill, but also on the rhythm inherent in the music to which you are dancing. A Scarlatti sonata and *I Got Rhythm* may be the same speed. They should not be treated the same way rhythmically (and of course not in movement). The melodic line will suggest accents and sequences. Listen to it before deciding on your rhythmic structure.

Advanced dancers, when using fast jazz, will find it valuable to use steps which make what I call cluster rhythms, which are analogous to grace notes in music. They have no assigned time value for each note or tap, but they must finish on a demonstrable beat of the music. Some of these steps can produce from eight to eleven taps. Do a series of them, beginning on a strong beat, let the accents fall where they may, and pick up the beat of the music the next time around. It's like coming out of a four-wheel drift in a sports car. This is really difficult and demands a very sure sense of rhythm. So does anything you want to do well.

Soft shoe and rhythm dances

We're now talking of speeds which range from twenty-five to forty-five bars a minute. Into this area fall most soft shoe and rhythm dances.

For a soft shoe dance (which isn't done in soft shoes—the term refers to the tempo of the music and its relaxed character), the most effective basic pattern is a series of eighth-note triplets— that is, three sounds to each quarter note, twelve to the bar, or the familiar sixteenth and a dotted eighth, which is the sound made by a succession of slaps.

The former is particularly good, since it blends with the easy flowing movements that are a part of soft shoe dancing. Accents should be used very sparingly, and continuity of even sounds should be the aim. Strive for this continuity no matter what step you are using to produce the triplets. This means that heels and toes should be used with a conscious effort to make the same sort of sound that you make with shuffles and ball changes. There will always be a slight change of accents as you vary the steps which make triplet rhythms. This will make sufficient change within this pattern. Don't let triplets become sixteenths and dotted eighths. They often do, because of one's natural desire to remain longer on a loud sound or to remain in the relatively safe gravitational position of having a whole foot on the floor.

Another effective soft shoe rhythm is to begin a simple step with a cluster of grace notes which start on the 4 of a preceding measure. Any step which makes from five to eight taps can be used. Follow this with two slaps (a sixteenth and a dotted eighth) and repeat. Make the accent following the grace notes a strong one, and do the slap very delicately.

Now I should like to introduce you to what I call diminished and augmented rhythmic sequences. Start with a rhythm of three sixteenths in triplet form followed by two sixteenths. Begin on 1, and put the accent on 1. This makes five sounds to a quarter note (shuffle, pull-back, [change] ball-heel, for example). Do four of these, one on each count for one measure. Follow this with a measure of eighth note triplets, then a measure of sixteenths and dotted eighths. Then step two quarter notes on 1 and 2 of the fourth measure and, beginning on 3, repeat the first rhythm to end on 4. As you can see, we have used fewer sounds in each measure, with a minute recapitulation at the end. This particular example took four bars. The theory may be applied to any length of phrase and with a succession of any sort of rhythms, provided each one in sequence makes fewer sounds than the preceding one.

Augmented rhythm is just the reverse of the above. Dynamically it is advisable to begin loudly and end softly, though this pattern can vary. These two rhythmic sequences are an important part of the rhythmic structure of tap dancing. Work on them.

There is a well-known step called the "essence." It is so named for reasons that are beyond any research I have been able to make. Its rhythm is valuable in soft shoe. It goes: sixteenth, dotted eighth, sixteenth, dotted eighth, sixteenth, two eighths in triplets, dotted eighth, sixteenth. The down beat, 1, is the first dotted eighth. It could be written: and 1 and 2 and 3 and a 4 and. This would make sense only to a dancer who knew the step. It is an example of the ambiguity of the general practice in counting. There is no ambiguity in the first method shown. In any event the rhythm is a pleasant one and can be done in many steps other than the "essence." It is especially valuable as a preparation for a phrase in sixteenth notes.

A final word on soft shoe. A soft shoe break is usually a very complex rhythm, but don't overlook the fact that sometimes complete silence is very effective in a break. And never use a break if it disturbs an already existing rhythmic pattern. A dance is a dance, and its rhythms should be disturbed only to create new areas of expression and communication, not to fit within hackneyed patterns.

If your dances do just this, you might resolve to break the mold. You'll be pleasantly surprised.

11 3's and 4's

Rhythm in tap dancing is a complex and unending problem. The fact that it is without end is fortunate, since it means your imagination need never exhaust itself for lack of material. The fact that it is complex is less fortunate for most of us, since it means making an effort, and a surprising number of people don't like to make an effort. It involves concentration on what is to be understood, and a conscious withdrawal from the habits into which most dancers have fallen or been led.

I should like to begin with a simple example which contains principles that are of value in the solving of all rhythmic problems. It is to understand the difference between a sequence of eighth notes and a sequence of eighth-note triplets and to be able to make either pattern at will. This is basically simple, though I have found that it causes difficulty.

An eighth note has half the time value of a quarter note, so there are eight eighth notes in a bar of four quarter notes. A bar of four quarter notes is usually referred to as 4/4 time, and comprises most of the popular music you will encounter in student tap dancing. A sequence of eighth notes is counted "1 and 2 and 3 and 4 and 1 and 2 . . ." etc. It is important to make the counting even. Each number coinicides with a beat of the music, and each "and" divides the time interval between the beats exactly in half. When you are quite sure you understand and can count the rhythm of a sequence of eighth notes for, let's say, four bars, make this rhythm with your feet by doing a waltz clog: step R, shuffle L, step L, step R, slap L, shuffle R, and so forth. Let's break this down and find out exactly what happens. Remember that a shuffle is made of a brush forward and a brush in, and that a slap, in this instance, is a brush forward and a step.

2 bars of eighth notes	Waltz clog
1	Step on R
and	Brush L, forward
2	Brush L, in
and	Step L
3	Step R
and	Brush L, forward
4	Step L
and	Brush R, forward
1	Brush R, in
and	Step R
2	Step L
and	Brush R, forward
3	
and	Wait
4	

The difficulty that seems to arise is that the weight shifting accents of the step do not match the strong beats of the music ("1" and "3"). The weight-shifting in the waltz clog occurs on "and 3" in the first measure and on "and 2" in the second measure. (It would be on "and 1" and "and 4" on the third and fourth bars if you continue the step.)

Now tap dancers have a great love of shifting weight, via a ball change in this case, and stopping after the shift is completed. They are, in fact, so eager to arrive at this gravitational haven of respose that they rush the first part of the ball change so that the "and" of the "and 3" is shorter than an eighth note, and the "3" is longer than an eighth note. Doing this will lead to a rhythm that will fit *East Side, West Side* very nicely, but it won't be a sequence of eighth notes, and it won't be the step I have described.

"Eighth-note triplets" are a musical convention which gets around the fact that the time value of notes in music is built on a geometric progression: 1, 2, 4, 8, 16, 32, 64. There are no thirds, sixths or twelfths. When such rhythms are desired, a

composer indicates it in a special way. He writes out three eighth
notes (in the case of eighth-note triplets), puts a semi-circular
line over the top of them and writes the figure "3" over the line.
This means that these three notes are to be played in the same
amount of time that would normally be given to two of them.
Thus, to indicate twelve evenly spaced notes in a bar of 4/4
music, you would write four sets of the three eighth notes with
the line over each set and a "3" over each line. A tap dancer,
to produce the same effect, counts: 1 and a 2 and a 3 and a 4
and a. Each quarter note is divided into three equal parts, as
Caesar did Gaul.

Now take the same waltz clog and make it sound in even
threes:

2 bars of eighth-note triplets	*Waltz clog*
1	Step R
and	Brush L, forward
a	Brush L, in
2	Step L
and	Step R
a	Brush L, forward
3	Step L
and	Brush R, forward
a	Brush R, in
4	Step R

The accents of a waltz clog done in this rhythm always fall
in the same place. If you begin with a "step" on 1, the next
waltz clog will begin on 3, the next on 1 of the second bar, and
so forth. This sounds as if it would be very easy to maintain the
rhythm of eighth-note triplets. It isn't. The same desire to rest
at the end of a ball-change manifests itself in this rhythm as it
does when you are doing even eighth notes.

If you refer to the description of the waltz clog in triplet
rhythm, you will notice that the ball-change takes place on "2
and" (and on "4 and" if you continue the step). Now 2 is a

weak beat, but it is still stronger than the "and" which follows it. Your instinct will be to rush the ball-change so that it finishes on 2 instead of on "and." You will then wait out the "and" and begin again at "a 3." This will produce a rhythm, but not the rhythm of eighth-note triplets. So be careful to restrain your eagerness to finish a ball-change.

There is another instinctive action which comes into evidence in trying to produce even rhythms. This is the desire to brush forward on a strong beat. It probably stems from wanting to "kick out" at the whole arduous business of becoming a dancer. Its emotional release may be valuable. Its mechanical effect is to distort the rhythm of this particular step. The brush forward of the shuffle in eighth-note triplets tends to coincide with the strong beats on 1 and 3, instead of the "and" following where it belongs. The step may continue to sound correct to you, but you will be one beat ahead of where you should be, and will consequently finish on the wrong foot when you complete the phrase.

When you have fully mastered the control of shifting from even eighth notes to eighth-note triplets while doing a waltz clog, you should apply the same principle to other more complicated steps. (For the Old Guard read: "shifting from 1 and 2 and 3, etc., to 1 and a 2 and a 3.") A good exercise, and also a valuable step, is to do a series of alternate wings with a battement. Let's see how it looks written out. In eighth notes:

The count	The wing exercise
1	Step R (croisé forward)
and	Brush L (to as high as you can, but straight)
2	Scrape R out
and	Brush R in
3	Land on R
and	Brush L in as you lower it
4	Step L
and	Brush R
1	Scrape L out

The count	The wing exercise
and	Brush L in
2	Land on L
and	Brush R in
3	Step R
and	Brush L
4	Scrape R out
and	Brush R in
1	Land on R

And so on for eight bars.

You will find this hard to do slowly. Either select a fast tempo or do the step in sixteenth notes (double time).

Same step in eighth-note triplets:

The count	The wing exercise
1	Step R
and	Brush L
a	Scrape R out
2	Brush R in
and	Land R
a	Brush L in
3	Step L
and	Brush R
a	Scrape L out
4	Brush L in
and	Land L
a	Brush R in
1	Step R

And so on for eight bars.

You will notice that in this step the strong movement, the "step" before the wing, coincides with the strong beat in the music—i.e., 1 and 3. This was not the case when the step was in eighth notes. Be aware of this difference in the relationship between dancing and musical accents. In this awareness lies one of the greatest attributes to good tap dancing. If you are aware of the sound you want to make and how it relates to the step you are doing and the beat of the music, you will always appear sure of yourself while you dance. Nothing upsets an audience more easily than the vague impression that the dancer—you—doesn't know quite what he's doing. Inversely, nothing so encourages them to accept you as your own conscious purpose clearly expressed. Don't make your rhythms by rote; make them by loving intent. This is more difficult to learn, but much easier to live with.

12 Acquiring technique and rhythm

The most difficult of the questions I am asked is: *How did you acquire your technique?*

This should be easy to answer. Every dancer knows how long he has studied and how hard he has practiced. If you add up the hours and multiply by the effort, the result should tell how you acquired whatever technique you may have. But it isn't that simple. Many dancers study for years and practice every day and still do not possess the technique they would like to have, or that would make them suitable material for a professional career. (Assuming, of course, that you have had good training from first-class teachers, and have not practiced faults.) What is it, then, that makes the difference? I don't really know. I only can outline what I think may be the causes.

Let's start by investigating the meaning of the word "technique." Does it mean the ability to do any step in the vocabulary of your chosen field of dance? Does it mean that you can do a limited number of steps with consummate ease? Does it mean that you can dance beautifully before an audience and excite them, or does it mean that you shine in the classroom and never make a mistake? Just stating the questions shows how complex the subject is. The dictionary says "technique" is the method of performance, especially as it applies to an art form. This isn't really a very satisfactory answer, and leaves a vague impression—as a dictionary so often does. Let us say, as a basis for discussion, that technique in the dance means you have so mastered the physical tools of your medium that those tools are not noticeable as such—the audience being aware only of the dancer and the dance, not of the steps and movements.

In tap dancing this means that every movement used in any step must be practiced by iteslf until the will and the resultant act are as nearly together as nerve and muscle response make possible. There is no conscious decision to do such and such a movement; there is only the conscious decision to dance a certain dance or variation.

How does one go about this? As an example I'll tell you about learning to do wings. After I had struggled through the initial phase of holding onto chairs so that I could support my weight on my arms, I began to do them unsupported on the floor. I would do about fifty of them on one foot, and then on the other. I would follow this with wings changing from foot to foot with a grand battement of the free leg. This I would do a hundred times with varying arm patterns. I did this every day for about ten years. I don't do so many in practice now, but I do many more in dances than I used to, and perhaps forty to fifty in various new patterns every day. I find that if I don't do this the wings begin to show an effort, or I may miss some altogether.

In the case of simpler steps like slaps and shuffles, I put them into combinations such as waltz clogs and essence steps and improvise for about half an hour. I change rhythms and accents to avoid falling in love with some particular sequence. Herein lies a serious pitfall. It is most seductive to do a certain step continuously in a certain way. You soon gain such complete mastery that doing it in any other fashion is a letdown, and soon you just won't do any other form of it. That is the beginning of the end. Be careful.

To follow the above outline throughout a complete vocabulary of tap dancing means about six to eight hours a day, and I hardly think the average student wants to do that. If you do less you'll learn less, and you know it. There are hundreds of thousands of students, but mighty few dancers.

So much for a brief outline of the physical work involved. I haven't even mentioned the hours of exercise necessary to develop leg, arm and body movement. They are common to all forms of dance.

There are two more essential parts to acquiring a tap technique. The first is being able to keep time and develop a sense of rhythm. I fear that keeping time is an innate quality, and either you can or you can't—like being tone deaf or color blind. Keeping time is an essential tool of the dancer. If you can't do it, then accept the fact and find some other medium of expression. But if you can keep time, then there is hope that with great effort and constant work you can develop a sense of rhythm, even if you have only a very slight perception of it at first. It's like not having a sense of humor. Humor is a product of environment, an observing eye and ear, and a quick, associative imagination. It can be practiced. Rhythm can be practiced almost constantly, though it may drive your friends crazy. Any regular cadence affords the background. The faucet drips; the taxi meter ticks; footsteps fall, so does rain; your heart beats. Whatever keeps time lets you practice rhythmic patterns without limit. In your head, or with rings on your fingers and bells on your toes.

How do you know if you're learning anything? You know by the increasing ease with which you understand any rhythmic problem presented to you, and by how well your steps sound. You can also tell by the fact that you'll be more successful and make more money.

The third and last part about acquiring technique is this: When (1) you can command the steps without conscious effort, and (2) have developed a sense of rhythm, you (3) have to put them together so they look good, like a dancer should.

A great deal has also been said about rhythm as a function of dancing, and as an entity in itself. Now, the effective combination of the two.

First a brief review of some important points concerning rhythm. It must be clearly understood that it is not the same thing as keeping time or having a good beat. Rock 'n' roll has a beat, and any decent orchestra playing it keeps time. Yet it is rhythmically more arid than the Sahara. Rhythm consists of visual or aural patterns which live within the framework of the beat and the time. This fact must be consciously realized by any dancer who wishes to emerge from the ranks of mediocrity. Emerge!

Begin by listening to music which has a rhythmic pattern. Or by reading poetry and prose which has rhythmic patterns. How can you tell? I could make a list for you, but in this case I think empirical methods will be more valuable. Just listen and read. Try not to be misled by accepting an intriguing beat for a rhythmic pattern. Start with early Beethoven sonatas, many of the Shakespeare sonnets, the Modern Jazz Quartet, Peggy Lee, some Stravinsky, Andrew Marvell, Shelley and Shelley Mann. And legions more. And don't overlook painting—the eye can help the ear. Lassetta, El Greco, Van Gogh, Picasso and Klee. All these use rhythm. Listen, read, and look. If you really do, you should be able to develop an appreciation of the function of rhythm in art.

In acquiring the technique of steps you can practice just exercises, or you can combine steps with good rhythm, and then you have to dance. If not whole dances, then at least phrases long enough to make quite clear to yourself and an audience just what you are attempting. Suppose you begin with what is called soft shoe dancing. (Bear in mind that you are not creating a dance, which calls for a great deal more than we are discussing here—you are practicing the acquisition of tap dancing technique.)

Soft shoe generally is in medium-slow tempo and has a melody with plenty of open space. *Tea For Two* is the classic example. First decide on what sort of physical mood the music and the tradition of soft shoe seem to call for. It is a plastic and smooth movement. It travels. It extends without apparent effort. It stays close to the floor without great vertical change. It turns, quietly. Now think of what rhythmical patterns would best combine with the music and with that sort of movement. I think you will agree that eighth-note triplets and the doublet of a sixteenth and a dotted eighth make a good basis. You don't have to use these, but you must select a definite pattern and stick to it. The sound of triplets is made basically by step, shuffle, step, shuffle, etc., and that of the above doublet is made by slaps. With this in mind, make up a phrase of continuous rhythm without doing a step. When it satisfies you, make up a movement phrase of the same length. Now see if you can match the rhythm and the movement without distorting either. If, for instance, the large movement of a wing with a grand battement is how you would like to move, and the rhythm you have made up for that section is in eighth-note triplets, don't change the rhythm to sixteenth notes so that you can do the wing faster and more easily. Instead practice doing the wing more slowly till you can do it with the sound you had in mind. Or if you want to turn with a shuffle, pull-back, ball, toe, don't make it a cluster of five sounds just because that's how you learned it. Rather practice it deliberately in the rhythm of eighth-note triplets until you have mastered the step—instead of being mastered by it.

This same method applied to all sorts of music and dance ideas will help you acquire a fluent and sure technique beyond what any amount of classwork or step practice can do for you.

The late great cycling Campionissimo Fausto Coppi, when asked his advice on how to become a champion, said: "Simple. Ride a bicycle! Ride a bicycle! Ride a bicycle!"

1⑬ Summer scholars

With apologies to Thomas Paine, I should like to dedicate this chapter to the proposition that dancing is an all-seasons, all-weather campaign and a love without end. Its conquest brooks no intermittent assault nor inconstant wooing. The spoils of a seldom victory vanish quickly without steady replenishment.

But the summer is a holiday. What better time to study?

And conventions are the clearing house for the oh, so valuable material for next season. What better place to learn?

The better time is always, and the better place is wherever you are and can make use of your sinews, bones, muscles, and head.

I am suggesting that you rely more on yourself. The responsibilities of a dancer, student, or teacher are great indeed, and it is difficult to find time, or even inclination, to pay court to the muses.

Let me review the inconstancies in each department and offer some possible solutions.

The dancer

Who has not heard the cry "If I could only get a job and make some money I could take class every day?" Indeed you could, and the discrepancy between the possibility and its realization is a matter of willpower; or perhaps the decision about the relative values of taking class or doing something else, particularly after a late night. In this realm I can offer little help; see your ancestors and early environment. I do know that the security of working makes it more difficult to study and practice. You work. You

have it made. Especially if it's a long time between jobs. The
visions of being carried out of the theater on the shoulders of an
admiring audience so becloud the real scenery that an objective
view about your dancing becomes almost impossible.

There is, however, another area in which the working dancer
often misses an opportunity to advance himself, and it has very
little to do with the conflict between the dream and the reality,
or the intent and the act. This is in the professional dancer's relationship to the choreography that directs, and limits, his dancing. It is seldom that someone else's choreography will exploit
your best steps. You don't do good extensions; the dances are
full of extensions. You do great knee slides; there's not a knee
slide in the show. But you mustn't worry about not being able
to do what you would like to do. Be consciously aware of
another person's favorite movements and do them, even if you
don't do them well. If you have a solo spot you won't be faced
with this problem, since that dance will naturally be made to
suit your own style. But in everything else you can help yourself a great deal by not allowing dissatisfaction to turn you into
an animated puppet. A real awareness of alien line and movement can help you more than you would imagine. Don't just
work on the things you can or can't do. Work on the parts you
don't like as well. Don't try to make subtle changes to suit your
skills. Become skillful in the original. You may never have to do
these particular steps again, but you will become a better dancer
by doing them. And you will be studying all the time you work.
Make use of what you have to do rather than letting what you
have to do use you.

The student

Students are divided roughly into two classes. There are those
who study because their families think they should do something
outside the academic school curriculum, but who have no real interest in dancing. And there are those who really do want to
dance. It is the latter who are most often guilty of the fairweather

approach. The serious desire to dance is often an excuse for not devoting as much time and effort as is necessary. In case this sounds contradictory, I ask you to consider how often the serious student comes to look on the teacher as a priestess-goddess-parent and the dance classroom as a cathedral. The teacher and the school are in some instances responsible for this attitude, but more often it is the student who creates the images. In so doing the student limits the process of learning by not relating to what is outside the classroom. When the teacher and the class become the full repository of dreams and hopes, one's own responsibility assumes a minor role. The summer sun and gentle breezes of study under much-loved tutelage can make one unaware of the inclement weather outside. But it is outside that you learn to dance. A teacher can show you what to do. But the meaningful use of this knowledge is the product of your realization of your total environment, everywhere and all the time.

The teacher

The case of the teacher fits the thesis of summer scholars more aptly than that of either dancer or student. This is so because teachers usually stop teaching entirely during the summer months and go to conventions to study.

And it is true they learn new things, and quite likely increase their skills. But material and technique are only one facet of a teacher's needs. Much else is necessary, and much of that can be worked on year round.

For example, what do you know about anatomy? Most dance instruction is concerned with the shape rather than the structure of things. There are muscles and tendons in most unlikely places that play an important part in specific movements and poses. It isn't enough to tell someone to lift or bend or stretch if you can't help them by explaining just what bones, joints, muscles, ligaments and tendons are involved. I am not suggesting you take a post-graduate medical course or become an anatomist, but there are relatively simple books with excellent

illustrations that can be most helpful. There are now several related to dance, but in most you must figure out the relationship
between movement, fulcrum, and tension for yourself. A nodd-
ing acquaintance with engineering principles is very valuable. I
suggest you buy a set of anatomical charts and try to remember
your school physics. Thus equipped, lift a leg and think about
it. Think about it hard enough to be aware of every part of you
that is working in order to do it. This can profitably occupy you
for many an evening.

But now back to the classroom. You will find, as your
knowledge increases, that you can add to the oft-repeated phrase
"Now feel as if you were hanging from the ceiling by a wire."
You will be able to tell the student just where the other end of
the wire is attached.

When you do a shuffle, is it the ankle bone, the leg bone,
the thigh bone, and the hip bone that are involved, or just some
of them? Or maybe more? And what about the leg you're
standing on? What lovely and precise adjustment takes place to
keep you from falling over? In being able to tell a student what
happens inside, as well as how the outside should look, you will
find much reward.

Have you listened to much music? You have read in previous
chapters that an understanding of music is an essential part of a
dancer's training. But how many teachers can help give this to a
dancer? Is the music you use composed mainly of melody, or
rhythm, or a combination of the two? Or may it be made of
either with equal validity? What is the difference between long
hair and short hair? Why is some music easier to dance to than
some other music? And, please, what is rhythm? And why is
"1 and a 2 and a 3 a and a 4 a and a 1" a limiting way of describing rhythms, particularly in tap dancing? Would the second
movement of the Debussy String Quartet be good to dance to?

Those are just a few of the questions you should be able to
answer. No records for class can furnish them for you. A skillful accompanist can help, but the real knowledge can come only
from your own labors. It will require an investment of a small
amount in literature and records, or at least a radio. But the

principal work material is you and your time, without stint. Any sort of musical appreciation and understanding is better than none at all, and a lot is better still. Again, I am not suggesting you become a Toscanini or a Dizzy Gillespie, but I do think a dance teacher must know a great deal more than the average person about music, that untiring and ever-present partner.

It is not essential that a teacher be able to dance brilliantly, but it is essential that a teacher be able to create the image and spirit of good dancing. There are many excellent teachers who cannot lift into a high arabesque but who can so beautifully show the line and structure of one that no student can fail to understand what it should be. To be able to do this you dance as much as you can and stay in as good condition physically as you are able. Even the spirit of a step demands the expenditure of considerable energy. So dance with your class when you can. This is, of course, more practical with an advanced class than an intermediate or beginning one. And watch your students. When you see a line you like or hear an interesting rhythm, don't just point it out—emulate it. Allow yourself to be shown as well as to show.

If you do these things you will find yourself making up more dances of your own. In any event, you will find that your studies are increasing—summer, winter, autumn, and the spring, too.

14 Your feet

The light touch

Being light on one's feet is a desirable characteristic whether one is a dancer or not. For the tap dancer it is not only desirable, it is essential. A heavy-footed tap dancer is a contradiction in terms, since "tap" means to strike lightly.

Being light is a matter of control and strength. Control, in order to place the weight-bearing leg or tapping foot exactly where you want it; and strength, to make sure you can lower the weight exactly when you want to.

Let us begin with the tools of the tap dancer, since they play an important part in producing lightness and clarity. The taps must be small and securely fastened to the shoes. There are small, light taps, and they can be securely fastened to the shoes. It takes more time, but it's not impossible. The same goes for shoes. They must fit, give support and be flexible. This costs more money, but it is not an extravagance. The best shoes are made to order. Ready-mades that will do can be found; it means more shopping around, but a serious dancer can find a good shoe.

The ankle must be very strong and very flexible. Constant exercise helps. For example: rotating, flexing, relevés, picking things off the floor with your toes. Exercise isn't a substitute for dancing, but should be done regularly no matter how much you dance.

The knees and thighs must be prepared to accept weight and sudden effort at all times, and be aware of the fact that they are doing so. The weight must exert its force in a straight line from its center to the weight-bearing portion of the foot; or, if the weight force is exerted angularly, it must exactly match the frictional resistance of the foot on the floor. If it doesn't you'll slip and fall—heavy or light.

The awareness your leg has of being about to receive the weight of your body probably plays the most important role in being light on your feet. I can't tell you how to practice knowing exactly where your well-pointed foot is in relation to the floor at the near end of a leap, but I can tell you that, if you want to land lightly, you must know. When you do, you can absorb the shock of landing with the minimum kerplunk, and you will sound almost as if you had stepped instead of jumped. The lowering of the heel plays an important part in tap dancing. Suffice it to say that the more you can control the lowering, the better. This requires strength and concentration.

The buttocks, the lower back, the lower hips, and the abdomen all help regulate the positioning of the weight-bearing legs. In order to be light on your feet, this area must control itself so that it is never unwittingly moved off its axis by the action of a leg. In other words, make sure you keep your hips down and in line when you do battements—little or large—at the barre.

The whole back works to keep your center of gravity where you want it. If you let it fold up to absorb the impact of a step or jump, the result will be more kerplunks, as well as being dreadful to see.

The arms and shoulders help to balance the rest of the body both physically and esthetically. They must move consciously and never be flung about—as is too often the case. Balance is not maintained haphazardly by frantic or desperate means. It is maintained by very exact and delicate adjustments, and when successful is a component of what we call beautiful.

The head must move so that the eyes always have a fixed point of focus. From this point the eyes can inform the brain how to order all the rest of the body to do the things discussed above. The head performs another function: it creates the overall point of view of the dancer, without which no amount of strength and control means anything.

Finally, remember to try to move "all of a piece" when you dance, and don't leave anything behind. It'll rattle if you do.

The tender foot

That dancing is a man's game was the theme of a Gene Kelly TV
show. In the exploration of this admirable thesis, emphasis was
placed on the analogy between sports and dance movements.

I think the program left unsaid one of the chief characteristics of manliness. I refer to the unique quality of the male for
tenderness and gentleness. So eagerly did the program present
the aggressive and tough qualities of the male, along with his
grace and beauty, that there was no time to include the tender
and the gentle. I would like to be presumptuous and do so here
in hopes of further convincing men that dancing is a man's game,
and that they need have no fear of appearing feminine in being
tender or soft.

Let us begin with baseball. Not only is the double-play full
of grace and beauty, but also it must be executed with the greatest gentleness. The throw is often but a few feet, and the ball
must then be scooped up from the infield. Throwing underhand
is considered a girl's way of throwing, but the exactness and
delicacy of this throw on the ballfield could be accomplished
only by a very strong and well educated muscle. Then consider
the bunt. A fine bunt is a masterpiece of controlled softness.

Have you ever seen a good soccer match between first-rate
teams? There was a soccer forward in England, name of Mat-
thews. He could run at full speed down a field and keep the
ball at his toe's end or within a foot of it for the entire length
of his run. He could kick it seventy yards if he needed to, but I
wager it takes more gentleness than any woman can bestow on a
babe to keep that ball at his feet while running.

Watch a top male golfer putt on a tricky green, and you'll
see caressing of a very high order. There are no women golfers
with an equally soft touch on the greens.

The forward pass in football is indeed a beautiful thing. But
the short lateral pass must be floated ever so gently for just a
few feet. Watching Johnny Unitas of the Baltimore Colts fake
two hand-offs before he finally got rid of the ball, you'd see one
of the softest touches ever.

The good male tennis players not only have a blinding serve, they also have a drop shot that falls like a feather. Women use a drop shot too, but I've never seen one return a hard shot as gently as a man.

Throughout all sports you will find examples of men outdoing women at what is thought to be a woman's specialty. There is one interesting exception that comes to mind. It is wrestling as shown on TV. Here is a sport which is ostensibly as rough and tough and manly as any sport can be. It is completely lacking in tenderness and gentleness. Yet, as it is shown on TV, it is utterly unmasculine. Its most popular manifestations consist of hair pulling, face gouging and simulated viciousness. With apologies to the ladies, these are largely the characteristics of a fight between women.

Now let us examine how men behave in fields other than sports. The greatest pianists can all play fortissimo, but the most tender pianissimo is achieved by the male (and most often written by him as well). It takes more strength to play softly on any musical instrument. And to sing softly.

Have you ever seen a surgeon operate? His hands, his manner and his presence have sureness and strength, and are of a gentleness to make one wonder.

In every field of human activity there is a similar pattern. The male is not solely distinguishable by his ability to hit the ball or his fellow male out of the park. Nor, in fact, is he distinguished by his participation in sports at all. The male is distinguished by his ability to take care of the ever recurring challenges of staying alive in a hostile environment, and by his ability to make valuable comments about how he does it. (Ladies, your indulgence, please—without you he wouldn't care about staying alive.) These abilities require him at different times to be fierce, strong, brave, hard and cunning; sweet, gentle, tender and loving. When a man dances, he dances about these abilities in those ways. His similarity to other athletes (a dancer is one) is based primarily on the fact that the body can function only in certain patterns. The expression of exuberance, be it in high jumping, ice-skating, or dancing, brings the same muscles into play. The motivation, somewhat limited in sports, is without limit to the dancer. A man's game is bigger than any playing field.

Your own two feet

This is a reiteration of a plea I have made before and hope to make again. Its premise is that your feet and legs are what you stand on, and you ought to.

Tap dancing technique is fundamentally simple. To learn its elements requires very little strength, very little sense of rhythm and practically no imagination. On the other hand, strength, a sense of rhythm and imagination are three of the things a dancer needs most.

Muscles grow with constant use, a sense of rhythm develops with effort and understanding, imagination expands with the search for and acceptance of challenge in new areas. Dancing without these things leads towards atrophy in body and spirit. If you are satisfied with atrophy, the material you are being offered at some dance conventions will help lead towards it, too. Those who are putting together the material they sell you are not stupid. They will give you what you want and deserve. If you think showing a ten-year-old something cute is more valuable than showing him how to dance, then you'll get the cutest routines you ever dreamed of. If you think counting 1 and 2 and 3, etc. is a valid substitute for learning what rhythm is, then you'll count until the cows come home and all the sheep are over that fence. The cows and sheep go on forever, but they don't do off beats at a fast tempo or jump five against eight. Only human beings can learn to do that. Being born human is a very remarkable advantage. Use it.

As soon as you do you will find that not only will you get more exciting material, but also that your own two feet are stronger and more agile than you realized. So much so that you'll be able to make up a great deal of your own material.

Here is an example: Step-brush is a pretty basic combination in tap dancing. Step forward on ball of the left foot and brush the right foot forward in the same direction. Let us make the rhythm "and 1." Step on "and," brush forward on 1. Now, how high do you lift the leg that makes the brush? Probably about six inches. Let's lift it higher. Step, brush and bring it about a foot over the horizontal. It is more difficult to lift it that high and keep the knee straight and the toe pointed, but you can manage it. What has happened to the supporting leg? It's likely that it has bent a little at the knee. The tendons in the back of the leg need stretching, and the muscles in front, which hold the knee (thigh muscles and quadriceps), need strengthening. Perhaps it would be better to begin the step in more of a plié. So, step forward on the left and plié before the brush. This tends to lower the heel. Let's lower it completely and make a sound with it; step, heel, brush. Now the rhythm is "and a 1." Now increase the size of the forward step to get a better start for lifting the right leg. Let's exploit this and make the forward step a slap. Thus: slap, heel on the left into a deep demi-plié and brush the right up to a foot higher than horizontal as you relevé up on the left. This makes four taps: "a, and, a, 1."

Let us see how this looks now. Yes, the upper body is strangely out of line. It is either bent forward or it leans backward. If forward, the lower back muscles need strengthening, and, if backwards, the abdominal muscles are weak. Now do the step with everything in line. Slap heel forward, brush, up and hold it for one and a half counts and step on the "and" before 3 and step left on 3, bring the left up behind the right in soussous.

Was anything lacking? Well, the arms didn't do anything. Arms help indicate the character of a step. Classical or jazz, they show the mood. They are controlled by the shoulder girdle and they have formally set positions from which you can depart whenever and wherever you like, so long as you mean to do so deliberately. And then there is the head. It is used in relation to the body and to direct the face, your very own individual face.

This is a very simple example of what you can do with a simple step if you will let it lead you to a complete exploration of its possibilities. Use this method in any combination. You will find more "material" than you can ever buy and not only will it be free but it will constantly enrich you. You'll better understand what Hippocrates meant when he spoke of how short life is and how long art is!

Over your feet

There are few things in tap dancing which do more to detract from its potential than an unbalanced body. An unbalanced body is usually the result of a leg movement which has been made in such uncontrolled fashion that it leads the body into imbalance. This lack of control results either in an excess of kinetic energy (kinetic energy is the product of mass and velocity), which literally throws the body into an untenable position, or in placing a strain on the joints and tendons which they are unable to support.

The development of stronger muscles will delay the moment at which the body becomes unbalanced, but it will not prevent the imbalance if either of the above-mentioned occur. Perhaps I should explain that by an "unbalanced body" I don't mean that you're going to fall over every time you arrive at it. I mean that your next move will be forced by the original movement, instead of by the intent and purpose of the step.

Let us begin with a very simple step, in this case back slaps. Beginners very often do these by sticking one foot out in front of them, swinging it backwards, practically falling onto it, and immediately sticking the other foot out to the front to help maintain balance. Sometimes this initial effort is not sufficient, and a speedy repetition becomes necessary. A succession of these movements, which began, remember, as back slaps, results in a sort of upstage, reverse off-to-Buffalo, and only the back wall will save you.

Now, if this same beginner would stand with feet together, lift one foot about two inches off the floor beside the other foot, raise the toe of the lifted foot from the ankle, lower it sharply to strike the floor, let it bounce up again from the ankle, move it to the back, step on it firmly and shift the full weight onto it, ready to repeat this sequence with the other foot, he would soon be doing back slaps with ease and clarity.

It sounds complicated. It is complicated. Any dance movement correctly done is complicated. More so to learn than to do, however, which is a saving grace. The essential factor in that description of how to do a back slap is learning to stay over your feet so that your balance is maintained on a firm base.

Another example, slightly more advanced, is pull-backs and a ball-change. These are often done by almost falling forward and just catching yourself before doing so. The end position includes a back bent so far down that the head is in danger of making sudden contact with the floor. Here not only the kinetic forces of an unbalanced ball-change, but also weak back muscles play a part. Try standing up straight before you begin the pull-back, bend the supporting leg at the knee, spring up, do the pull-back, and land on the other foot in the same position you started from. Keep the lower back muscles under tension and the free leg relatively straight behind you, so that you are in an arabesque at the end of each pull-back–ball-change. Keep doing this till you are quite sure of being able to land firmly on one foot with your center of gravity as nearly over that foot as you can make it. Then add shuffles or brushes or whatever you like. Staying over your foot in this step will give you a new lightness and ease in all variations of pull-back.

Another very common pitfall in this area is the one which confronts the beginner in doing wings. In this step the initial effort is made to the side with the supporting leg, i.e., the leg which is going to do the wing. The beginner will let this initial movement throw his body away from the direction of the winging leg, and will tend to fall away from the wing. To maintain balance he will have to land on his winging foot long before it has had time to scrape out to the side and brush in. In order to compensate, the body must not lean away from the wing; if it leans at all, and it may, it must lean into the wing. In other words, it must stay over the winging foot.

If you are doing wings with grands battements of the free leg, you have two forces to contend with: the forces generated by the wing, and the force generated by the rising leg. Here you must take care to balance them exactly, and neither be thrown to the side by the wing, nor backwards by the battement. You should just move up and down over your center of gravity.

It is very easy to let your legs dictate your movements. Try to remember that your legs and feet are part of you, and that you are the dancer. You control your legs; your legs must not control you. The difficulty of making sounds will often obscure this fact, and lend you the gracelessness and gaucherie which are so traditionally associated with tap dancing. Help destroy this tradition.

15 Tap tour

On October 12, 1959 in Rockland, Maine, I began a concert tour of some forty cities in the U.S. Appearing with me was Ellen Martin, who has danced in some industrial shows, been most delightfully entertaining in night clubs, and studied hard and faithfully with me in New York. (See what happens when you go to class every day!) At the piano for us, and doing two groups of solos, was Robert Kaufman, who studied at the Eastman School of Music in Rochester, and at the Juilliard School in New York. He has never danced a step in his life.

I hope you will be interested in reading about some of the things that happen on tour to a very small tap dance company like ours. First, something about the program. I begin with two tap dances to classical music. One is the gigue from Bach's *B-flat Partita*, and the other is a four-part Handel suite from his opera *Alcina*. This consists of a minuet, sarabande, musette and tambourino. Then Ellen follows with a dance to the third of the seven Beethoven *Bagatelles*. After that I do a short improvisation which isn't on the program at all and I'll explain why later. A duet to *Greensleeves* follows this. We do it as a sort of ancient blues. This old English folk song is, in fact, one of the first torch songs. Bob Kaufman plays some Chopin very well, and I follow with a *Sonata for Tap Dancer*, in four movements, without music. Then Ellen and I do a very short Caribbean dance with music by Forrest Wood (who played for my classes in New York). This brings the first half to a close.

After the intermission Ellen and I dance a modern blues. Bob plays another group. I do a dance to *Tea for Two, In a Dance Hall,* and *Political Speech.* Ellen and I do a jazz number, and we end the show with an ad lib in which Ellen joins.

So much for the schedule of the performance. I mention it so that you will have a clearer idea of problems we face from time to time.

All the dances have some sort of lighting, varying from medium full-stage to a dim blue spot, or to a bright centered area and a red stage—not complicated, but needing about an hour's rehearsal with an average lighting set-up.

We are doing this tour by car—a very fine station wagon that does about everything except the laundry. I am driving. The tour covers about ten or twelve thousand miles, which means a lot of hours in the car, requiring that it be both comfortably soft on the straightaway and firm on corners, without sway. If you've never tried dancing within an hour after a 350-mile drive, you have no idea how even well-trained muscles can act as if you'd never danced a step. Fortunately this wagon takes less out of you than any I've driven before. The make is withheld at the request of General Motors and Ford.

On October 11 we were ready to take off for the toll roads and turnpikes that interweave throughout the Northeast. Everything had been checked and rechecked. New shoes had been broken in, costumes packed into traveling bags, make-up renewed, suitcases stacked compactly in the back, and maps of practically every state sotred in the glove compartment. Ellen sat in front, and Bob squeezed into the second seat beside the costume bags. These were hung on a patented rod which was fitted near the roof of the car on the door frame moldings, and which was guaranteed to become more firmly fixed as more weight was applied. It appeared to do so till the first red light stopped us.

We then discovered that the rod was indeed well suited to support downward pressure, but had no resistance to forward movement. We extricated ourselves from the costume bags which inundated us and found that the fall had made all the hangers inside the bags jump off their retaining bar, and the costumes were all piled up in the bottom of the bags. This meant pulling over to the curb, taking out all the costumes, putting them back on their hangers, and putting the hangers back in the bags. We

then set about refastening the rod. This took rather longer than
the directions suggested, since when it had fallen off it had separated into its ten or twelve convenient, chrome-plated, easy-to-
fasten-together parts. In turn, some of these, like washers and
turn screws and such, had gotten under the floor mats. We finally did reassemble it, and hung everything up again. Since this
took the better part of an hour, and we were only four blocks
from our starting place, with four hundred miles to go, our initial excited optimism over the beginning of an adventure was
somewhat subdued. True, we planned to arrive in Rockland the
night before the concert, so there was time to spare, but dinner
at friends had been arranged, and a smooth trip had been hoped
for. The rod was finally secured and all seemed well.

About fifty miles up the parkway a most annoying thing
developed in one of the wheels. I had fitted the car with very
expensive and much better tires than those originally furnished,
and I was most upset that one of them was evidently somewhat
out of shape. The thump stayed with us, but got no worse, and
we made Rockland in time for an excellent dinner.

The next day we set off in the early afternoon to rehearse at
the auditorium. We were booked by Community Concerts, a
division of Columbia Concerts, and nine out of ten dates use the
local high school auditorium for the performance. So I auto-
matically went to the local high school, unloaded costumes and
bags, asked the secretary where the auditorium was, found it,
and started in—only to discover there was a dramatic class in ses-
sion and we would have to wait until 3:15 to use the stage. We
waited. When the hour arrived, we entered and looked on a very
tiny stage and a very old piano. We were dismayed but un-
daunted, and started to figure out ways of making the dances
smaller and, if possible, tuning the piano. We had been at this
for about one hour when the school secretary, with whom I had
spoken earlier, came in and said there was a phone call for me
in the office. I followed her, picked up the phone, and learned
that the concert committee and stage crew for our show had
been waiting for over an hour for us at another auditorium, and
were wondering if we had gotten lost or just weren't going to

show up at all. I didn't dare try to explain and just said we would be right over. I went backstage and shamefacedly repacked everything and carried it to the station wagon. We said goodbye to the secretary, and never did find out what she thought we were doing at the high school in the first place.

Finally we arrived at the theater. The stage was large, the lighting equipment looked splendid, the piano was a beautiful concert grand, and the committee was beaming and eager to forgive and be helpful. Bob sat down at the piano, Ellen and I put on practice clothes and shoes, and stepped onto the beautiful, new-looking stage. It was slippery as wet ice.

Yes, you could slide right across the stage with very little effort, and it was only about two and a half hours before showtime. There are ways of taking wax off a stage, but very few keepers of an auditorium like to use them. A stage looks very pretty when it has a high sheen.

Happily, lye, hot water and soap were found, and we all scrubbed. The result was a stage we could dance on, and arms and shoulders that were very well warmed up—but legs and feet which had little time for their share of limbering. This necessary part of a show was even further delayed by a light rehearsal and instructions about the curtain and the front spot.

One thing above others is quite certain about touring on the road—one must let people do the things around a theater that they have learned or been told to do. It is hard to realize that though *you* perform about five times a week, the crew of any high-school auditorium has a chance to strut its stuff only three or four times a year. It would be merciless to make their tasks appear less important than your own warm-up. After all, to them you are a professional who must be ready to go at a moment's notice—practice is for amateurs. I digress. We did get warmed-up and made-up and ready.

The show started, and all went well until Ellen Martin finished her delightful opening dance and I suddenly became aware that I had programmed *Greensleeves*, a duet, to follow her solo. Ellen had a costume change which in some mysteriously absent-minded way I had never once thought about when we rehearsed.

So I went out front and said so. I also said I would improvise a dance with Bob Kaufman's improvised music (this was the first he knew about it). I began to do so when, by frantic signs and sounds from off-stage, I was made aware that Ellen had been locked out of her dressing room, and no one could find the key. It was finally found, and Ellen was able to change, but my dance was a record length for improvisations.

The next few dates produced no special moments or slippery stages. The car ran beautifully, the hangers stayed on their supports, we managed to squeeze in a little rehearsal time, and felt very pleased with ourselves. We also became reacquainted with that inescapable companion of the traveling artist—the reception after the concert.

The civic-minded hosts are invariably friendly, delightful and eager to assist you in any way they can. Their care of the outer man is impeccable, but sometimes the finger sandwiches and cookies fail to nourish the inner man. A dancer dares not eat a meal *before* the show.

One of the difficult problems on the road is to find a restaurant open in a small town after the reception. In fact, one of the problems of a touring dancer is to find a restaurant—period. Outside of big cities, the staple diet appears to be fried steak, fried potatoes, frozen orange juice and ice cream. We fervently hope the health of the nation is better cared for in the home than in those ubiquitous establishments lit by erratically flashing neon signs which spell out EAT.

Back to dancing. As we moved farther west, the jumps between dates became longer, and we found ourselves spending six or seven hours on the road on the day of performance. This left very little time for rehearsing, and made it necessary to figure out an accelerated warm-up program. The edge of an open grand piano makes a very good barre, and precisely because it is of obviously great value, one holds it very lightly.

Pliés and pliés are the basis of a warm-up when you haven't much time. These, a few ronds de jambe, and grands battements done away from the piano, with a slap-heel-brush, are the requisites. Then about a hundred slaps, fast ones, as many step-shuffle-steps, a few wings and some deep stretches must generally complete the pre-performance exercises.

Stage space is often a problem, since auditoriums vary greatly in size and shape. Whenever you come across a particularly small one, you are almost always told that the Yugoslav National Folk Ballet, with a company of thirty, played there.

Everything continued to go smoothly for us for two or three weeks, and we had uncrossed our fingers about our routines, our ankles, our shoes, concert committees and the car. We were on the last day of a hop in northern Nebraska. Roads were long, rolling, and utterly deserted. We hadn't seen a town or a car for sixty miles. It was mid-afternoon. We were approaching the crest of a gentle slope. The motor quietly sputtered dead, and we coated to the top of the rise to view an uninterrupted 360 degrees of unbroken horizon. I pulled to the side of the road on our remaining momentum, and broke the news to Ellen and Bob that we were out of gas.

We looked and we listened—no trains, no cars, no nothing. I thought of putting my ear to the ground in hopes of catching hoof beats. As I began to do so the lovely silhouette of a huge double-decker diesel truck appeared on the horizon. I waved as if we had been on a desert island for months, and he rolled to a stop. There was a friendly response to our predicament and I climbed aboard. The cab was huge. There were two drivers and a bunk for sleeping. There was also a swing-down card table. Solitaire, I guess, since truck driving is a full-time job. These drivers were hauling ninety-four herd of cattle to market. We talked of cattle and show business and found much in common.

They let me off at a gas station about eight miles up the road in the direction from which we had come. The station was run by a gentleman weathered and creaking, as was his model A Ford, but he closed his station to drive me back to the car with a five-gallon can of gas. He said he'd been born and raised right there, and had never been more than thirty miles away in his seventy years. Never had no mind to, either.

We made our show easily. It was in Lead, North Dakota, a town which still makes gold mining pay, and is haunted by the memories of rich men who came, gathered it in, and fled. It no longer pays much—the mining, I mean—but the town makes up for it in warmth and hospitality. We went on the next day to Montana. We did four dates there, some more on the way to the West Coast, and stayed in California for some fifteen concerts. Not only was the weather what the Chamber of Commerce says, but also you could get a drinkable cup of coffee, which we hadn't had for some time.

Stages to perform on varied from small to non-existent. This last sometimes meant dancing on a gym floor without curtains, and with only the overhead lights for lighting. They were either on or off, and when they were on it made a great deal of light— cold, bright light. Dancing a blues with Ellen, a blues you hope is lit by the torch you're dancing about, in a light like that makes you feel very silly. You do it anyhow and the audience is very nice about it.

The entrances and exits are about eighty feet from floor center so you show the people an imaginary set of wings and drapes and they accept it most cooperatively. There's a hand whenever you cross the line either way, and make-believe has a life of its own.

A few days later we had an almost unfortunate meeting with an officer of the law. He had stopped us, with reason I must admit, and called me out of our car to come back to his patrol car. As he began recounting my sins, past and probable future, two large stray dogs leaped out of the brush at the side of the road. They rushed eagerly towards me and bayed in frenzied delight as if they had found a long-lost master who had never fed them anything except calf liver. I made a few feeble efforts to act as if they weren't there, realizing that there was a prior demand on my attention, but soon found this impossible and gave up. The dogs smothered me in bounding love. The officer regarded the three of us for some time and then shook his head. He muttered something about no man being all bad who . . . and wrote out a ticket for the smallest infraction he could think of. I shall always remember his courtesy and regret I had no liver for those splendid dogs.

We went on to do eight shows in succession, and were more than ready for two delightful days in San Francisco. This is a city which grows ever more beautiful, outside and in, and we were refreshed in body and spirit. I bought a camera while I was there—a very fine single lens reflex made in Japan.

Now toward Los Angeles, did several concerts on the way, and arrived late one evening to a most garish array of neon lights, filling stations, and giant jumbo super malts.

On to the fabled town of Twenty Nine Palms. So you thought it was only a song? No, the lady in the song might have come from a real place. It is not yet a major city, but it exists. And a fine winding road up into the hills takes you there. This was another gymnasium set-up, but there was a stage and curtains and wings. The audience was seated on the flat floor, but those in back gradually stood up, since it was difficult to see the stage from a flat floor.

There was a set of folded-up bleacher seats down one side of the gym. It made a ledge about five feet high and two feet wide. Many people scrambled up and sat on this ledge. Almost all of children did. I could see them, since they sat in the front seats. As I finished *Tea for Two* and was talking about the next dance, I noticed one young lady, about nine years old, who was having a very hard time trying to reach the top of the folded bleacher seats. She appeared to be hanging rather precariously in midair, and I sprang to the rescue. The stage wasn't very high, and she wasn't very far from it. I explained to the audience as I ran, and was at her side in a moment.

"There, there," I said soothingly, "I'll have you up and safe in a second." I grasped her firmly under the arms and lifted. She seemed to struggle rather strenuously for some unaccountable reason, but I had a firm grip on her, and am a good deal stronger than any nine-year-old girl. I seated her firmly on the ledge and smiled in anticipation of her thanks. "There we are," I said. "Here I am, indeed," she replied, "and now I'll just have to start climbing down all over again."

My pride forbade me helping her down, since I feared she wanted to leave the show, and I made my way sorrowfully back to the stage and explained this development to the audience. Sure enough, she lasted one more number and then vanished to greener fields.

By now we had done about thirty dates and were on the home stretch. Our performances were becoming very smooth. Ellen and Bob gave flawless performances, and the only mistakes were mine. Ellen was so skillful she would sometimes make the same mistake with me, and lent me great comfort as well as covering up my errors. It was very difficult to find enough time to practice, and though we knew our dances we found that practically all other technique had departed. There is no substitute for daily class and practice.

A few days before the end of the trip we found ourselves in mid-Texas. We were all in excellent health and had escaped inclement weather. I felt brisk, energetic, and only sorry to be nearly through with the tour. I discovered I had no vitamins left and went into a drugstore to buy some. The clerk was a small and feeble man of about sixty-five who could barely make it from the shelf to me as he searched out the formula I had asked for. He looked serious, reached over, patted me on the shoulder, and said: "I think these will give you the lift you've been looking for. Goodbye now, and take care of yourself."

On this cheerful note I realized the time had indeed come to end our tour and this very brief account of it.

1⑥ Some notes on the waltz clog

The waltz clog is one of the most useful and maligned of all tap steps. The maligning begins with part of the name itself. The word "waltz" stands for graceful music and flowing dance movement. The word "clog" is harsh in sound and conjures up a vision of walloping accents in heavy, thick soled shoes. The step very often sounds like that, too.

I don't think I need describe the waltz clog—I'm sure all of you know how this basic step is done. I will say that instead of starting with a step, shuffle, ball-change, I start with a slap, shuffle, ball-change. This maintains an even rhythm and is more flexible in variations than stopping at the end of each ball-change.

It was originally done to waltz music and still can be, but not, except in a satirical vein, to a waltz such as *East Side, West Side,* etc. Choose a decent piece of 3/4 music—a Strauss waltz or a classical minuet, and start with very even and clear eighth notes. It is very important to make each beat as short and sharp as you possibly can. The movement remains gracious and fluid (I shall describe it fully later) but the sounds must be staccato. The secret of sharp taps is to maintain as short a contact with the floor as you can. If your foot slides as much as an inch, yes—even an inch, the sound of the tap will be slightly blurred. Try and develop such flexibility and strength in your ankles and feet—and such control in your thighs that a shuffle–brush out, brush in, becomes two distinct downward beats of your toe on the floor; one done as your foot brushes out, the other as it brushes in. Do a slap so that the step after the brush is as short as, and no louder than, the brush. This means stepping only on

107

the ball of the foot with the heel well raised. Many tap dancers let the heel drop, perhaps unconsciously, when it shouldn't and a slight blur results no matter how softly the heel is lowered.

Practice till you can make six perfectly even beats in each 3/4 bar. Don't try and make sure of an accent on "1" until you have achieved evenness on all the counts. When you can do this, try making a slight accent on "1" then on "2" and then on "3." It is most essential to be able to accent any tap you choose, instead of being limited to accents which result from putting your weight on a particular step.

The arms start in second. You begin on the left foot, the right arm moves to the left and across the body as the right foot does its shuffle. The body leans to the right and a slight but definite plié is held throughout the step. The right arm moves back to second on the ball change, (through) and the step repeats to the other side. The changing of arms and the leaning of the body must be done very smoothly. The taps should sound light and sharp.

If the music has any air of nobility about it, a nice variation in arms and body is to relevé to an almost straight leg on "1," lift right arm to fourth position as right foot shuffles "2," return arm to second and plié distinctly on "3." Repeat on left side. Resist the temptation to make "1" or "3" strong beats—keep all the taps even.

Now, doing a waltz clog to 3/4 music is very good exercise but it is not the most practical use you can make of it. Most tap dancing is done in 4/4 time. (This isn't necessary. It just happens to be so because it is the line of least resistance.) The waltz clog is very valuable with 4/4 music. With exactly the same step and the same movements described above as the basic form of the step, there are three rhythmic patterns you will find useful. The simplest one uses a medium slow blues beat and would usually be described as "a 1, a 2," etc. The second basic rhythm is again in a slow 4: 1 and a 2 and a 3 and a 4, etc. These will be written as eighth notes with a triplet sign over each group of three, shortening them so that twelve notes will fit in a 4/4 bar where, strictly speaking, there is room for only eight. The third is simple double time in which every tap is a sixteenth note. Since the step has six taps in it you can amuse yourself by figuring out how many complete steps each rhythmic pattern would need in order to finish on a "home" beat: that is a "1" or a "3." When you have done this, remember that you can stop the step whenever you like, on any beat, without waiting for the much loved goal of most tap steps, the ball-change.

A nice exercise consists of doing two bars of each rhythm and finishing the eight-bar phrase by returning to the first pattern. Make the transitions where they come rhythmically and don't try and start each one as the beginning of a waltz clog step—they won't come out that way.

Another exercise is to use the brush out of the shuffle as the "1" count and continue from there. Start this slowly as it is more confusing than it sounds. Use it in all the rhythmic patterns I have shown you. The object of these exercises is to give you confidence in using your feet with the same facility that a pianist has in his fingers. Tap dancing seldom exploits the fact that your feet are yours to do with whatever you want and they can. The accents do not have to be where the weight is placed. Home is not always standing still. Home is wherever you have enough imagination to live.

17 A tap barre

In order to facilitate the use of the body, arms and legs in tap dancing, and to develop the muscles necessary for this use, I have made up a series of exercises at the barre that I find very helpful.

All other forms of dancing have a warm-up and exercise period, generally at the barre, before starting the steps in the middle of the floor. I think tap dancing should have one as well. It usually doesn't, for two reasons: first, because it is generally considered that tap dancing is performed solely with the feet, therefore there exists a certain embarrassment in using, or preparing to use, other parts of the body. Secondly, because of the fascination, in tap dancing particularly, that "steps" have for a dancer. Learning a "step" is an achievement. All else seems secondary and an obstacle to progress. Steps are indeed important, but they play the same part in dancing that a tube of color or a brush does in painting. They are basic, but they are not dancing. If you disagree with this premise, don't read any further.

I think good tap dancing needs the same fundamental control and strength that is necessary in ballet or modern technique, plus a special development of the feet and of the rhythmic sense. Here are some of the preparatory exercises I use in class and for myself whenever I rehearse.

Stand in the middle of the floor with legs in a moderate second position. Do a porte de bras in all positions, exaggerating the width of each movement to stretch arms and shoulders. Do deep bends to both sides and forward and back: rotate the shoulders front to back and reverse. Rotate the trunk, twist and bend in all directions, such as the famous horseman rode off in. In other words, stretch all of the upper part of the body until you glow. This before going to the barre.

111

At the barre, do the regular pliés. With pliés in second, I generally add heel taps rhythmically, like this: 1, and 2, and 3, and 4; for the full plié, repeat this coming up.

Now for the battement tendu. There are many tap variations with this exercise. For example, from fifth position, slide working leg forward and tap once with pointed foot, being sure to keep leg and foot in stretched position. Do this with two and three taps, do not let the ankle flex, and return leg to fifth position. Another variation is to point forward, one tap, and step heel into fourth position plié, straighten back leg, point working leg again to floor, one tap, and close to fifth position, step heel, two taps. The accent may come on the heel in each plié: and a *1* and a *2*, or on the point: *1* and a *2* and a *3*. These exercises should be done front, side and back, usually eight times in each direction.

Battements frappes: From a sur le cou de pied position brush forward and straighten leg and foot, one tap, being sure to stretch the foot as much as possible, return to a sur le cou de pied position. There is one tap sound made by the brush. Then brush side, return to sur le cou de pied in the back, brush back, etc. This exercise starts slowly and it can be done up to any speed you can handle, taking great care that the leg and foot are straightened when they should be, and the sound is clear. Try not to kick yourself in the shins or the ankles as you return the working foot. You can also syncopate the rhythm of the movement in any desired pattern such as "1, 2, 3, 4, and 1, and 2, and 3, and 4."

Shuffles relevés: Stand on half toe and execute a series of shuffle balls front, side and back. Do this as fast as you can, while maintaining a clear sound of "and a 1, and a 2, and a 3," etc. I should like to add here a word of warning as to what the word "back" means. It means just exactly that, and not at an angle of forty-five degrees between the side and the back, as it is so often performed. To be more precise, the shuffles to the back are performed by brushing directly to the back for the "and," brushing forward from an extended position in the back for the "a" and stepping to a close fifth on the half point for the "1."

An exercise for the strengthening and coordinating of heel and toe: Stand on left leg in a demi-plié, left hand on the bar, facing forward. Bring free leg, well turned out, to a sur le cou de pied position, point toe as strongly as possible till it points directly downward in a line that bisects the supporting foot. The toe should be an inch or so from the floor, the heel forward, and the leg turned out. Raise the heel of the left foot, without lifting the body, bring the heel down sharply and touch the toe of the right foot to the floor, keeping the foot pointed, and repeat. Do this in triplet rhythm, and very fast, 1 and a 2 and a 3 and a 4, to seven counts.

Lift right leg to the back on eight, and repeat the same exercise, taking care to keep well turned out or the foot will not pass closely enough to the supporting leg. There are many variations of rhythm possible. This exercise may also be done with the right leg moving slowly from front to back in the form of a rond de jambe à terre.

Battement fondu développé with heel beats on supporting leg. Perform this exercise in exactly the same way that you would perform it in a ballet class, but add a series of rhythmical heel beats with your supporting leg as your working leg does développé in each direction.

Grands battements: Left hand on the bar, stand on right foot, left foot pointed to the back in fourth position. Bring left foot forward with a slap, finishing on heel. Raise right leg to grand battement position, lower it, step heel, extending the left foot to the back, as you plié on the right. Repeat eight times, and then perform the same exercise to the side and to the back. This exercise may also be done with relevé on the supporting leg each time it finishes the slap heel sound. The sound, incidentally, is "4 and a 1, rest, and 3."

A very good exercise for developing strength and speed of the feet is as follows: Standing on one foot with the other foot in a sur le cou de pied position, tap the free foot on the floor as long and hard as you can. Take care not to bend the knees nor to motivate this movement from the thigh. It is done solely from the ankle, and can be done slowly or fast or in varied rhythmical combinations; be sure not to allow it to become what is called a "nerve tap." It must be muscularly controlled.

These are some of the exercises that I consider essential. I can promise you that a faithful performance of them daily will improve any tap dancer's technique, in both skill and speed, to such an extent that all ordinary steps will seem ridiculously easy. This, of course, does not happen overnight or at the end of a week, or at the end of a month. Good dancing like any other creative effort needs the sharpest and keenest of tools and an unceasing dedication to the education of one's muscles, tendons, head and heart. It takes a long time.

Advanced exercises

The above has dealt with a tap barre in its fundamental aspects. I should like to describe in more detail some of the advanced exercises which I find to be the most helpful in acquiring a good technique.

Having finished the battements and stretches we now proceed to: face forward, left hand on barre, stand on left foot in plié with foot facing forward parallel to the barre, not turned out. Right foot is extended à la secondé with toe pointed; right arm in second. Wing on left foot, landing ball heel, and at the same time développé forward. Repeat the wing and développé to the side, and to the back and continue for four sets of sixteen wings and développés on left foot; repeat on the right foot. (The count is 4 and a 1, 2 and a 3, etc.) Be sure that the upper body and free arm remain relaxed throughout. A port de bras may be added once the coordination of feet and legs has been achieved.

I should like to stress here the avoidance of a very common fault I have noticed in the execution of wings. Wings are often, if not always, done more like a pull-back than a wing. There is a slight sideways flick of the foot and an immediate backward movement which results in a back slap, an unbalanced landing and a slow but steady retreat from the audience. Don't do this. Be sure that the winging foot returns to the identical spot from which it started.

Second exercise: Facing the barre, développé onto the barre with right leg, plié on left leg with foot forward at a right angle to the barre. Take hands off barre, place arms in second and do a series of wings on left foot, being sure to keep extended leg straight on the barre with toe pointed. Repeat on right side.

Third exercise: Face barre. Stand on right foot, left foot sur le coup de pied in back. With hands on barre, shuffle ball on right foot—and a *1* and a *2*—continue sixteen times on right and sixteen on left. I think you will find it helpful to put some weight on the barre, since this step is more difficult than it sounds. It can also be done landing on the heel and with the addition of a toe tap after the heel, making five sounds in all. The toe tap should be done first to the back and then to the front, making the change by means of a clean high passé.

Fourth exercise: Face barre, hands on barre, stand on the toes of both feet with knees bent and do the above exercise with both feet at the same time, or almost at the same time. One foot should slightly lead the other, so that there are six distinct tap sounds. Breaking it down: first, you are in the air with both feet off the floor; then, brush left forward, brush right forward, brush left back, brush right back, land left, land right. It takes much more time to read this than to do the step, which by its nature is quite rapid.

There is another good exercise connected with wings at the barre that you should practice. Face barre, hands on barre, stand on right foot, scrape right to side in exactly the same way you would use to start a simple wing, then do a shuffle and return to starting position. This is a four-tap wing: 1 and a 2, 3 and a 4. The accent is on the landing, 1 and a 2. Do eight on each foot. It is not easy, but it is very valuable as a means of developing strength and articulation in wings of all kinds.

The exercises I have described can be done on the floor without the barre, and should be so practiced, but only after the student has mastered them at the barre. The object is not only to enable the dancer to learn the steps, but also to develop a complete control of independent foot movement and rhythmic facility. As your tap dancing advances you should be able to choreograph more and more from the basis of movements of your body, arms and legs in space and over the stage, and still make the sounds and rhythms of your choice, instead of being limited to movement which is dictated by the sound of the taps. Dancing is primarily visual—the taps are an added ingredient.

18 A tap adagio

After warming up with a tap barre, you are ready for work in the middle of the floor. The exercises I find most valuable here are similar in form to an adagio, similar to those done in a ballet class, with the addition of taps. I do not recommend any set steps. It is more important to know the general principles from which the exercises are derived. I don't think I have repeated a step in this part of a tap class since I began giving classes. Many of the exercises begin with a fundamental tap step that is as follows: Stand on right foot with left pointed on floor in second. Slap left to fifth position in front of right foot, two taps, drop heel, one tap, and brush right foot to right, one tap, turned out and toe pointed. This may be done on either foot and from the front or the back as well. The right foot finishes with a brush in the opposite direction from that which the slapping foot starts. The down beat is on the final brush, the first three taps are pick-up beats: 1, 2, 3, *1*. I shall refer to this movement as "slap, heel, brush" in subsequent descriptions of exercises and steps, or even SHB, which is of course short for sh-boom.

Some exercises: Use music with a slow four beat. Stand on right foot facing diagonally to the right forward, left pointed diagonally to the left back, arms in fourth. SHB and continue the brush to a full extension; plié on left leg and développé right leg inwards and through passé to arabesque. Remain in demi-plié throughout this exercise and beat left heel in quarter notes. The movement takes two measures, eight counts. You may double the rhythm of the left heel to eighth notes. This exercise is repeated on the other foot, arms moved in any desired porte de bras. This can also be done starting with a SHB to the back and développé forward. Be sure that you remain in a demi-plié throughout and that the head and body do not move up and down. Using this basic design there are a great many adagio exercises that can be done. It is important to stretch the extensions to their utmost while executing smoothly the tap sounds on the supporting foot. This will help give strength and coordination.

A very good exercise is as follows: Stand on right foot—left foot extended and pointed on floor to left side. SHB and relevé on left as right leg extends to a full second position; count 1 (use the same tempo of music as before—a slow four) hold for second count in extension; bring right leg down in front step heel right and lift left to a coupé position in back, count 3, step on left, count 4 and repeat to the left side. This moves you forward. Repeat eight times, and then repeat going backwards.

Another exercise: Stand in fifth, left in front, slap left foot diagonally forward to the right, drop left heel, step right (1, 2, 3, 1), step right again as far forward as you can into a deep lunge on the right leg, straighten the left leg as you do this so that the inside of the forward part of the left foot is on the floor and there is a straight line from your left toe to your right knee. You are on your second count. The next six counts are done on the right heel while performing a deep porte de bras. On "1" of the third bar, begin a slow turn of the body to the left, remaining in the deep plié on the right leg, turn till you face left diagonal, left leg still straight but now the left foot is flat on the floor—this takes four counts—shift weight to left leg through a deep echappé and straighten right leg to the same position that the left leg held in the first part of the exercise. This takes four counts. The first two of these are on the right heel, the next two on the left. Continue tapping left heel and slowly rise on left leg, sliding right leg up and développé to front attitude croisé with right leg. This takes eight counts (quarter notes) and if my arithmetic is correct we have now used up six bars of slow music. From the extended position I have left you in, continue beating the left heel and begin a grande rond de jambe with the right leg to second position (four counts). From here do a slow reverse turn, relevé on left and finish on left leg with right in coupé in front. Repeat to the other side.

Throughout these exercises maintain as correct and extended a position as you can. Be sure that final positions coincide with final counts, and that the movements are as smooth as the tap sounds are staccato. Do not be perturbed that these are slow steps—it is only through such controlled movements that speed can be acquired without awkwardness.

There are many more exercises in controlled movement. Make up some of your own. Use those movements and positions in which you find yourself weakest, and avoid the things you do most easily. Or, if you must, use them as a dessert after the more solid food.

Make any heel rhythms you like on the supporting foot; change supporting legs with the SHB. Do promenades in arabesque; in second, in attitude, front and back. Use every extension to its limit and combine this with varied porte de bras. The object is not only to develop strength, line and balance, but also coordination of arms, body and sound, with the fundamental leg movements.

Two good exercises for balance are as follows: Slap heel on left in front of right and relevé as right brushes to the side. Remain in relevé position while doing shuffles front and back with right foot. The rhythm of the preparation is 1, 2, 3, *1*. The shuffles are performed with the accent out, and 2, and 3, and 4, for seven counts. Then slap heel on right foot, relevé right, brush left and repeat with left foot. The shuffles are the ones we do at the barre. They must be done in as turned out a position as possible, and they are not the relaxed foot flip-flap to which the word "shuffle" usually refers. They are a very distinct brush out, brush in, with the foot tensed and pointed. The other kind are often used, but not in this particular exercise. They can be done with the accent *in* as well as with the accent *out*.

Another excellent exercise for balance is this one: Stand on right leg, left pointed on floor to the back, croisé derrière. Slap heel on left, with a plié, and brush left to a fully extended battement in front croisé. Développé inwards remaining in demi-plié on left to fourth arabesque. While you perform this movement, the left heel beats eighth notes in triplets. The rhythm of the preparation is 1, 2, 3, *1* (as in the first exercise); the 1, 2, 3, are pick-up beats for the accent on the battement *1*. Then come the eighth-note triplets (twelve beats to the bar). The movement takes two measures of moderate 4/4 music. Stop on the third beat of the second bar and hold (in arabesque) one count. Repeat on the other foot.

Do this exercise on both diagonals and reverse it as well.

Here is an exercise for advanced pupils that I have found most effective for improving wings. I include it in the adagio section because it demands the sort of control and balance that adagio exercises are meant to develop. The wing movements usually turn out to be done pretty fast. Try to do them slowly. Here is the exercise:

Stand in fifth. Développé right in front, plié on left, and wing on left. Land with a step heel under control. This makes four even beats (scrape, brush in, ball, heel). Be sure not to jerk arms or shoulders (arms in fourth) and do not lower the extended leg. Développé to second and wing, développé to back and wing. Do this to a very slow four. Use three counts for the développé and one count for the wing. The full counting is 1, 2, 3, a and a 4.

I am going to describe a few preparations and endings for pirouettes. They are simple tap turns and lead to more complicated combinations. It is very important to learn them fluently. I am assuming that anyone reading this is able to do turns. The ones I use are identical with ballet pirouettes.

Stand in fifth, right foot in front. Extend right with a brush (1) to second, relevé (2) at the same time on left. Lower right drop on left heel and place (3) right to fourth in back with a step heel (three taps). Pirouette en dedans on left and finish on right in arabesque (step heel (4) two taps). From the arabesque, brush left to side, relevé on right and repeat exercise to the left. This may also start and finish with a slap heel (slow 4) but be sure to finish in arabesque.

A valuable preparation: Starting with a slap, do a forward wing, at the same time battement diagonally forward in écarté, finish with a heel drop on the winging foot and step heel into fourth position with the leg that has just done the battement. Pirouette en dedans and finish with a SHB. Repeat to the other side. Do the same exercise with a pirouette en dehors. As the back leg comes forward and around, do a shuffle (two taps) and finish in arabesque croisé (step heel).

On left, facing diagonally to the left, stand in fourth with right écarté derrière, arms in fourth. With right leg slap heel and brush, brush left leg high and relevé. Make a quarter turn to the right and finish with heel drop and plié on right leg and left leg développé in to point left foot in front of right toe. Arms have moved through fourth into preparations for an en dehors pirouette to the left. The count is 1 and a 2, 3, a 4. The written numbers are the musical count, a slow four. Now slap heel left and shuffle right. The count is 1 a and a 2, turn on 3, pirouette en dehors into arabesque croisé (a 4). Repeat on the other side.

Practice en dehors pirouettes with a continuous brush out brush in. Brush from the back to front, and front to back.

On all turns, whether you do one or ten, practice starting and stopping exactly when and where you decide to do so. In all the above exercises this is *on the beat*. Nothing looks worse than pirouettes that last longer than the musical phrases of which they are a part. Remember that in tap dancing not only the eye of the audience needs a definite framework, but also the ear. If you demand imaginative work on the part of your audience let it be in reference to your own creative imagination; not in reference to the tools with which you present the results.

19 Two tap combinations

I am introducing two combinations at this point as a relaxation from the hard work of acquiring a technique. They may prove to be something you can use in a dance or just to have fun with.

The first combination is the more difficult of the two. The start is downstage center. The music is a fast four in well defined rhythm. Either the *A-Major Toccata* by Paradies or *I Got Rhythm* in stop time by George Gershwin will serve as speed limits. The entire step is in a steady and clearly articulated series of sixteenth notes without change. It lasts for sixteen bars. The stage pattern of the step is a counter-clockwise circle finishing in a straight line down stage. Your own movement is explained below. Here we go:

Start: Stand on R, hop L, shuffle R forward, hop L, shuffle R to R side, hop left, step across L with R, drop R heel, slap L, slap R, brush L diagonally to L in battement, wing R (land on R and don't forget a wing has three taps: scrape out, brush in and land) slap L, and start turn to left as you shuffle R diagonally to the back (by this time, having started at 12 o'clock, you should be at about 9 o'clock), pull back L, land R, drop pointed L toe in back of R, drop R heel (continue the L turn during this), slap L, slap R (finish the L turn) and slap L. The final tap of the last slep L will start the repetition of the step. The arms begin in second position. They close in slightly during the "hop shuffle"; they open to second for the wing; and the R arm goes up to make a fourth position, with head slightly inclined to R, as you do the shuffle pull-back turn; they come back to starting position as you do the final slaps.

Repeat this three times, which should bring you around the circle, counter clockwise, to 3 o'clock. Begin a fourth repetition

and when you get to the slap R which follows the first heel
drop, do a series of four wings moving forward like this: brush
L diagonally to L, wing R, slap L back toward R, brush R, wing
L, slap R back toward L, brush L, wing R, slap L back toward
R, brush R, wing L and finish on ball of L, heel raised, L in plié
and R a little higher than sur le coup de pied with R knee bent.
Throughout this part of the combination keep the arms in a relaxed second position, your head straight, and move steadily
forward.

You will finish on the third count, a strong beat of the last
bar. You will have made 126 sixteenth-note taps—all even, all
clean, and without being misled by the fact that the step is not
symmetrical, that is, the same tap sound is not in the same
musical position in each repetition of the step. Just do what's
written and it will come out fine. Practice it on the other side
as well—clockwise instead of counter-clockwise.

The second combination has only steps—no slaps, pull-backs,
wings, shuffles or heel drops. The music should be very solid
jazz of the "rock and roll" type. A shade faster, if anything.
The step covers ground and each movement must be as strong
and large as you can make it.

Start: Stand about eight or ten feet to the right on the middle of the stage facing forward. Think of yourself as the center
of a clock face. Feet in a loose fifth, R in back. (Use a two bar
pick-up if you like.) On "1" slide into a deep lunge diagonally
to the right rear, R foot pointing to the figure 5 on the clock
face, weight well on R in as deep a plié as you can manage, L
leg straight, toe well pointed and aimed at 11 o'clock, R arm extended horizontally to 7 o'clock and L arm extended, croisé, to
3 o'clock. (Don't worry about being a few minutes early or
late.) The head is turned to the audience over the left shoulder.
Hold this position for 2, 3 and 4. With your stretched out left
leg only the inside of the left toe should touch the floor. On
"4" prepare yourself to pirouette to the left on your L leg, on
"1" of the second bar step firmly onto the left leg and turn.
The right is in sur le cou de pied in back. Turn as many times
as you like or can until the "and" before "3" of the second bar.

On this "and" step R, on "3" step L, and on "4" step R, with weight on R. You may continue the turn during these three steps, but be sure to finish facing front with R in front and legs straight. The three steps are done in plié and straightening occurs at the end. Arms are in second on "4." On "1" of the third bar lunge to the left with left leg in deep plié and right leg extended and straight. The right arm sweeps across to a croisé position pointing to 10 o'clock, left arm raised and head still forward over right shoulder. Hold this position with very exact stillness until "and 4" of this third bar. On "and 4" step R behind L and step L slightly forward to a diagonal fourth (10:30) position. Remain in plié and on the balls of the feet, heels well up. On "1" of the fourth bar step over L with R and brush L to L side on "and." This is a preparation for a jump to the side and must be done strongly. Accent the "1." Jump to the left, arms have come down during the preparation and now move to second position as you jump. In the jump, both legs should be straight as in an echappé. Jump as far to the left as you can on "2" head up shoulders down. Land L on "and" before "3" and on "3 and 4" step R, step L, step R in a sharply accented manner. The right leg steps in front of the left as you do this. The finish is in plié, heels up, head and arms alive, and any kind of smile except a cute one and be ready to repeat the combination to the other side. Do it four times.

Be sure you really sail when you do move and make the motionless parts full of the expectation of movement. Stillness in dancing without conscious intent of future action is deader than dead, just as action without intent to stop is silly.

20 Choreography for tap dancers

A dance, like a sentence, always has a subject and a predicate. Like most sentences, it usually contains an object.

Let's begin with a very basic subject and predicate: "I dance." That sentence is, I admit, simpler in English than in dancing but, carefully interpreted, it is the essential beginning of any dance. Think about your own value for "I." Examine it with all your powers of concentration and do not try to disguise the result of your examination. I am not suggesting a self-psycho-analysis—in spite of the do-it-yourself craze—I mean as objective as possible an outline of yourself as a physical entity and as a personality. Are you tall, short, hard, soft, lean or pear-shaped? Are you characteristically funny, sad, noble, cynical, gay, wise, dumb or a say-hey kid? The answers may not be absolutely ac-curate, but they will furnish you with a starting point for de-ciding on the "subject" of your dance.

Perform the same operation on your dancing style. What are the steps you do best? Is your style light, heavy, lyric, bop, or flat-foot? The answers to these questions will help define the "predicate" of your dance. More explicitly, if you come to the conclusion that you are pear-shaped, dumb and flat-footed, you will avoid attempting a fleeting dance to a fast Scarlatti sonata, though you may well do a first-rate hustle.

With this guide you can make up a simple dance—or can at least know what sort of a dance you should make up.

Now most sentences have an object as we stated earlier. "I dance a dance" is an example. In this sentence, the second "dance" is a noun. A noun is a symbol for some material thing

or for an idea. For choreographic purposes, let us define it as
representing an idea. I don't exclude the possibility of dancing a
"table" or a "match box," but that goes beyond the scope of
this chapter.

So I suggest, I implore, that when you make a tap dance you
have an idea behind it, or rather, in it. Make the dance "about
something." Nothing in dancing is so shatteringly empty as three
choruses filled with sound and fury and arms and legs and no re-
mote suggestion as to why.

Nothing is so meaningless as a series of steps without com-
municable motivation. It makes no difference how difficult the
steps nor how expertly performed.

Now the great problem—how to find an idea for a dance. It
isn't quite so tough as it seems. One of the advantages of being
born human is the ability to react to stimuli. Anything that happens within your being makes an impression on you. Any impression can result in an idea. Any idea can be the basis of a
dance. Is it exciting to you to keep time? Then use keeping
time as an idea for a dance. Does the title *I Could Have Danced
All Night* stimulate you to thoughts of what it would, literally,
be like to do so? Use it. (Condensed, please.) Does making
moan over lost loves occupy you with a consuming passion?
Then *mean* that when you begin to choreograph a blues. Does
man's spirit strike you as unconquerable? Hop shuffles can help
to say so if you believe it. Is the kid next door in the black
leather jacket an unbearably difficult character? Cut him down
to size in a dance.

There is an endless supply of ideas for dancers. The only
qualification is that the ideas by yours alone. If you do something because you think it's smart or hep or commercial, but you
don't really believe it, you can be sure only of mediocrity. There
is no make-up, costuming, arrangement, scenery or lighting ever
invented that can really disguise you. Who you are, how you
dance and what you dance about will always show through.
They always tell the truth about you. This, fortunately, is exactly what an audience wants to know. An audience will gladly

admire and express admiration for the feats of a performer who remains a stranger to them. But I think you will find they reserve their true love for those about whom they have discovered the most profound secrets.

Now that we've discussed how to make up a dance in terms of your own personality, your own dancing style and your own reactions to the world around you, let's explore how to select and arrange a musical accompaniment.

Classical and jazz

There are, very broadly, two fields of music: classical and jazz. Each of these has many sub-divisions. There is only one way to become familiar with the fields and the pastures therein. Listen to them. Listen to music. Listen some more. Listen alone and listen with somebody who has studied music. Find out something about the composers and the period in which they wrote. Discover some of the strains and stresses of the society they lived in. Become familiar with the development of polyphony and counterpoint and leit motifs. Not only is this valuable for a dancer, it is great fun for anybody. You will find plenty of the present explained by the past. This applies mainly to classical music, but you will discover that jazz also has its development and is far from immune to the influences of classical music. Become familiar with its phases and styles. Don't just be sent by the latest backbeat rock. Enjoy the added pleasure of knowing that "backbeats," "offbeats" and complex syncopations were effectively used by Beethoven and Brahms, too. Not that New Orleans was the direct cultural descendent of the romantic 19th-century composers, but rhythm belongs to rhythm and is not the exclusive property of any special modern jazz group.

Listen, explore and learn! You will find much music you'd like to dance to, music that fits the ideas you already have about yourself, your style and the object of your dances. You couldn't use all of it if you lived to be a thousand.

Choosing music

Here is how you make selection easier. The chief difference between tap dancing and any other sort of dancing is in the sounds
a tap dancer makes. You make them in order that they be heard.
So don't choose a piece which needs a hundred musicians to
play it. If you like both the *C Major Double Piano Concerto* by
Bach and also the *Prelude to the B Flat Major Partita* for the
piano, it would be more practical to choose the Prelude. It is
seldom possible to make piano transcriptions of orchestral
pieces. It is done and I have done it, but I don't recommend it.

If an arrangement by Dizzy Gillespie sounds wonderful, remember that the four piece band at the Silver Bell in Rubber
Boot, Idaho isn't going to be able to play it. So limit your selection to pieces that can be played by a pianist or by the bands
you are likely to be working with. If you want to use some
classical music, it is essential to have your own accompanist.
This is expensive, particularly when you are starting a career, but
if you can possibly afford it, do so. It saves hours of arduous
rehearsal, it leaves you completely confident and at ease when a
show starts, and it means you can choose your music from a
much larger field than would otherwise be possible. There are
hundreds of delightful pieces by Scarlatti, Bach, Couperin,
Rameau, Purcell and many others that are ideal for tap dancing
and are not too difficult for a pianist of average talents. You
can hear them on records or you can buy collections of them
for very little. Have them played for you and you will be sure
to find one that will have just the mood and tempo that you are
looking for.

Sometimes you will find that a certain piece will suggest a
whole dance to you—an idea you'd never thought of but which
suddenly jells as you listen to the music. Then the only work
you have left to do is the delightful love's labor of shaping that
empty space and putting the sounds where they sound best.

Where do they sound best? A good question. I shall try to
give you some basic principles. You can either follow the
rhythm of the beat of the composition or the rhythm of the

melody, or you can change from one to the other. In "following" you can put tap sounds exactly with the rhythms or against them. There isn't any place else for them to go.

By far the majority of tap dances are done to popular music even though this constitutes a much more limited field than classical music. There are a number of things to remember when you are looking for a thirty-two-bar chorus.

Be true to your music

Keep your basic idea in mind and try to find a piece which represents it musically. Then stick to it. Don't be tempted to add eight bars of another piece for a fast finish. If you want to do a fast finish, do a fast dance. If you decide you want to dance a blues, find a good blues and dance it, don't drag in a rumba to "change the mood." All that is indicated by an arbitrary changing of the music in mid-dance is that you didn't know what you wanted to do in the first place and are therefore wasting the time of the audience. They may applaud you but they won't really care.

Orchestrations

You will probably be working in a rehearsal hall with a piano player. If the dance is going to be orchestrated, think about the arrangement as you make up the dance. When the arranger arrives explain exactly what you want and why. If you don't, you'll hear seven brasses blasting in unison while you're doing nerve taps. Remember that an arranger is concerned primarily with how the music sounds from a standpoint of the instruments he has to work with—you must be concerned with not only the sounds of the music but also the musicality of your dance. If you want stop time and a certain phrase sounds great on the piano, then be sure it's done like that in the orchestral arrangement. You'd be surprised at how thunderous stop time can sound if it's played by an entire band. If the arranger says he'll give you a light rhythmic background, he will probably mean piano, bass and drums. This can make much more noise than you expect. A light rhythmic background is Jimmy Crawford using the brushes alone. Make this clear and you won't be left wondering what became of how it sounded in rehearsal.

Music is your partner

Above all, a dance is not a series of unconnected steps done because they are the only steps you know or because you think they are good steps and will excite an audience. A dance is a dance. It is a continuous, meaningful line of expression and communication. The arrangement of the music you dance to must have this same quality. It must start, it must go somewhere and it must finish. Music isn't an antagonist to be left wounded and bleeding as you beat your way through an eight bar tag with *a la seconde* turns. It is the most willing and the prettiest partner you'll ever find. It asks only to join you.

The dance

We have already discussed you: your subject matter and your music. I shall assume that you are now standing in the middle of a rehearsal hall with tap shoes on your feet, ideas in your head and music and accompanist at the piano. The floor around you looks very bare and your reflection in the mirror is motionless.

This is always the worst moment in making up a dance. Once you break this hard shell of inactivity you will begin to gather momentum and discover that you have done most of the hard work before arriving at this point. This means that you know what sort of a dancer you are, what sort of a dance you want to do and what music lends itself most equably to an expression of both these factors.

You ask the pianist to begin playing and you start to dance. Don't try to do finished steps and phrases. Just move around in easy steps—walking steps if you like. Become completely familiar with the melodic and rhythmic accents of the music you have selected. As you do this you will invariably find sections of melody or rhythm which will ask for special movements and sounds from you, in keeping with your overall concept. By "overall" I mean that you have already determined whether the dance is to be in a linear or circular or diagonal pattern; whether it is to emphasize high steps or low steps, flowing movement or sharp, separate phrases. Within this framework you will now find if you listen carefully and keep moving around, that you begin to do specific steps or at least the outlines of them at certain moments in the music. This must be done consciously and not by hoping for a lucky accident—though that does happen sometimes.

You may find that after having chosen a step for a phrase you are led to other steps for that particular part of the dance. Go right ahead—a dance doesn't have to be made up from the beginning. You may find it easier to start at the ending or the middle. Just be sure to remember where you are.

When you have a few such moments, begin to think of connecting them. If a step has carried you upstage right, don't forget that sometime you have to move out of there and go someplace else.

If you have a nice idea for your finish and it finds you downstage left you might do well to leave it there. There's no law that says a dance must end in the center of the stage.

In any event, to move from one part of the stage to another you must dance the distance and it is here that many dancers find themselves in trouble. Here are some general principles.

Rhythmic progression

Suppose that one of the steps that fits a high spot is in a fast double time rhythm. You can lead into it in one of several ways. (1) Begin with quarter-note taps, change to the familiar sixteenth and dotted-eighth pattern, then to a phrase of triplets (twelve eighth notes to the bar) and so into the double time of straight sixteenth notes. (2) Reverse this sequence beginning with the triplet phrase. (3) Begin with a series of large movements in half notes with no tap sounds in between and then suddenly begin the double time.

Select one of these patterns, don't just do a step and follow it with another step.

If one of your high points is an exciting syncopation it is best to lead up to it with a series of off-beat accents that prepare the ear for what is going to happen. As the end of a syncopated phrase be sure to reestablish a down beat—even if it is a very simple step—for long enough to relax the listening ear so it can appreciate what went before.

If a high point is a series of jumping turns with a flourish of grace taps before each step, it is valuable to do some sort of steady rhythm before you begin—preferably in a straight line. Conversely, in coming out of a spin a series of steps or jumps in a straight line is more effective than a turning step. Don't forget that the eye and ear of the audience can only absorb and retain so much. Most dances are far more complicated than they need to be.

Silence

Don't be afraid to accent a rhythm by absolute silence beforehand. It is often very effective to do nothing at all for a bar before a step. Don't move and don't make a sound, then enunciate a short step with decision and pause again. A rhythmic pattern that might well be lost in a shuffle will stand out when it starts from nothing.

Bass or treble

You can make up steps to either one. You can reinforce a sublety of tune or rhythm in your accompaniment or you can follow a strong lead of the same. Make sure that you know when you change from one to the other and try to do steps that will indicate your knowledge.

Steps versus a dance

As we have mentioned many times in this book, a dance is made
of a series of steps, but a series of steps do not make a dance.
So try to resist the temptation of doing a step just because it is
a good step. Be sure that you lead up to it and away from it in
sound and movement so that an audience is prepared and will
not forget. Above all, no step—no matter how spectacular—
should ever be done if it bears no relationship to the dance as a
whole.

Now all this may seem very sparse and insufficient. Perhaps
you are thinking or even complaining that I haven't told you exactly what music, what steps, what stop time, what high points,
what part of the stage and when. It's true, I haven't. If you're
going to choreograph your own dances nobody can tell you
these things. The best thing about being born human is that you
can remember, think, dream and act.

21 How fast can you dance?

How fast can you dance? A mile a minute? An inch a year?

There is no effective way to measure the speed at which a dancer can dance, and if you could measure it you still couldn't say whether it was fast or not. When you say something is fast, you are describing its rate of movement relative to some rate with which you are familiar. Fast is a relative term, not an absolute one, and there is no definition of "fast" as such. Speed can be defined. It is the measure of time necessary to move from one point in space to another.

The difference in actual speed between the battements or turns or beats of one dancer and another may be very slight, but one may look slow and the other fast. In fact, both dancers might be moving with equal speed and still give a different impression. The eye is a very inaccurate gauge of speed, even of relative speed, and other qualities of movement play an important part in the eye's estimate of how fast a dancer dances.

The tap dancer, of course, makes plea to another sense perception, as well as the eye, in giving an impression of speed: the ear. The ear is as poor a gauge as the eye for time measurement. Both need to be exposed to a high degree of definition and clarity in order to create anything like an understandable image in the brain. A series of wildly flung arms and legs may move with far more speed than good fouettes, but they won't look as fast because they will not be registered clearly by the eye. Control and duration are the essential qualities which a movement must have to form a lasting visual image. The eye will not easily accept a formless pattern. So the hours and hours of simple exercises, often boring and tedious, are not to develop speed per se, but speed in an appreciable form.

"How fast" implies not only "fast" but "slow." The good dancer in a finely executed jump looks not just slow, but motionless. This is a result of two factors: the speed with which body and limbs can place themselves in the peak shape of the jump and the length of time they can be held in that position before moving into the position necessary for a landing or the next step. Nobody "stops in the air a little and then comes down," not even Nijinsky. But they do move so fast before the "leap image" is achieved that the eye doesn't record the movement. It sees only the shape of the leap in the air. Likewise the preparation for a landing and the landing itself are not recorded— just the finishing pose. The effect is sensational.

A tap dancer should strive for this, even though he or she doesn't plan to spend a good part of his or her life in the air. Tap dancers have another element at their disposal by which to show how fast they can dance. How many taps can they make clearly audible in a given period of time? (It took long enough to get here, didn't it?) All right. You're dancing pretty fast if you can make fifty-six taps in five seconds. Taps, not blurred sounds. One of the best steps for sheer speed is the hop shuffle combination that goes: Hop L, shuffle R, hop L, shuffle R, hop L, step R, heel R, slap L, slap R, shuffle L, hop R, shuffle L, and so forth. Another is the waltz-clog combination with heels, slap heel L, shuffle R, step R, step heel L, slap heel R, shuffle L, step L, step heel R. With either of these steps you should be able to work up to at least a bar of 4/4 music a second, eight taps a second, forty in five. I have managed sixty-four taps in five seconds, but I don't guarantee or recommend it. A good exercise for developing speed is the very simple step, shuffle, step shuffle, step shuffle. Do this in four, that is, step 1, brush out 2, brush in 3, step 4, brush out 1, brush in 2, step 3, and follow on. I have stressed before and I shall repeat, it is the clarity and shortness of the sound that makes it heard. The long scrape isn't a sound, it's a noise. Visual and aural impressions demand careful delineation.

Neither of the steps outlined above call for much movement; they can be done in a very small space. A step such as wings with battements, however, calls for large leg movement. Speed in this step means not only fast taps but a very fast lifting of the non-winging leg to its highest point and a holding of it in that position till it must come down, to make the necessary sound. The step itself is slap R, brush L and lift L as quickly as possible and hold it as still as possible (for the eye to see it) while you wing on R. The left begins lowering after the scrape out (the one allowable scrape in tap dancing) brush in of the wing so that it is ready to begin a slap left immediately following the landing of the right foot which completes the wing. You should be able to do about fifty-six taps in six seconds. In this step that means you life your legs alternately nine times. That's a fair rate even without the wings and slaps. The toe must be pointed and the knee straightened during each movement or the movement will not register clearly as a step at all.

If the foot is slapping while the leg is in the air it will distract the eye from the leg movement and the speed won't look "fast" it will just look clumsy and inept. Think of this with all steps. Control of the movement and duration of the image are what give the impression of speed or stillness. (I am not discussing legato or continuous movement, an equally important but separate phase of dancing.)

To return to pure sound effects, here are two advanced steps. One consists of eight taps in a single step, about the limit so far as I know, and one is a continuous fast sound step.

Stand between two chairs in the familiar practice position. Support your weight on the chair backs and brush L out, brush R out, brush L in, brush R in, land L, land R, drop L heel, drop R heel. The best way of describing what the sound should be is a nice clean b-r-r-r-r-r-p. Now do it without holding on.

The other step starts in the same way. Hold onto the chair backs. Shuffle L diagonally to the back, shuffle R diagonally forward, land on L, drop L heel, shuffle R diagonally to the back and continue the pattern. Smooth it out to a regular rhythm of thirty-second notes. Now walk away and do it without chairs.

Both these steps will help your speed in all tap steps. But the root of the answer to "How fast can you dance?" lies in your dancing being measurable at all by those frail perceptors, the eye and the ear. If you can't be seen or heard, you might as well be standing still, off stage.

22 How to be a bad dancer

The usual means of becoming a bad tap dancer are so varied and so simple that it hardly seems worthwhile to chronicle them. But in the interests of those who really like to do things the hard way, I have decided to describe some of the subtler and more difficult approaches to the subject. Before I begin, I shall give a brief résumé of some of the well-worn paths—just a refresher course.

First on the list is not having a sense of rhythm. It is amazing how many dancers fall for this easy approach to the problem. Almost anyone can succeed here, and many do.

Next comes lack of coordination. This, of course, will make one a bad any-sort-of-dancer, but it is particularly fruitful in tap dancing. Since the legs perform many fast, small movements, uncoordinated body and arms are more noticeable. Lack of coordination is also an overcrowded field.

The third easy way has to do with facial expression. This form of being a bad tap dancer has a long and almost honorable tradition. It begins in a vacuum. That is, it presupposes that the dancer has no thoughts or feelings that bear any relation whatsoever to the dance. This being so, a series of feigned expressions are allowed to flicker ceaselessly over an otherwise empty face. These may simulate joy, passion, great pain, or immense surprise. They may follow each other in any order so long as they never relate to what you are doing. This approach has many staunch adherents who would use no other, but there is one serious drawback. The facial muscles often become so used to this exercise that they don't stop working when you stop dancing, and your friends may consider you the subhuman you look.

So much for the tried and true forms. Fortunately there are those among us who seek out innovation and are always eager to try less trodden paths. It is for them that I have selected some more arduous ways of achieving badness.

Let us assume that you eschew all the above mentioned easy virtues and their allies. You have rhythm, coordination, technique, and you are able to express what you feel in your facial expressions without resort to grotesquery. You're a good tap dancer and have no idea how to be bad.

One of the best ways is to overuse your skills. You can do this by dancing too fast, too hard, or too much.

If you are really skillful you can make about sixty-four taps in five seconds. This is nothing like as fast as a machine gun, but it is considerably faster than the average ear can assimilate with any degree of appreciation. A sudden short burst is often effective, but any prolonged display of such speed, which is exceedingly difficult, will almost certainly dismay and confuse any audience. Dancing too hard means, in this discussion, making too much noise in the right places. Rhythmic accents are essential to tap dancing, and a good dancer can use them easily and meaningfully. But one can, with diligent practice, plus performance excitement, over-emphasize the difference between the running tap sounds and the definitive accents. This sometimes leads to increasing the sound level of the running taps. The result is that you will produce noise instead of music with your feet, and the audience will retreat to a safer haven.

Dancing too much doesn't mean dancing too long. That frailty belongs in the first group of approaches to bad dancing. The good dancer never dances too long. He can, however, dance too much by constantly striving to add one more turn, or by trying to gain an extra inch in elevation. You can't do this unless you are good. It requires hard work. Once achieved it is an almost sure road to being bad. Your dancing will always have the slightly strained and uncontrolled look about it that will always prevent you from being considered at or near the top.

There are other, non-technical approaches worth investigation. One is the over-intellectual approach. Sometimes skills are so sure that there seems almost no way to harm them. Just try making up a dance, using all your skills, in which the subject matter evolves from such a cerebral base that it is understandable only with the help of a lengthy Baedecker. The audience has neither the light, time, nor inclination to read this in the auditorium, and what happens on stage will be a secret noun instead of a transitive verb.

This last is perhaps the most difficult course to follow, but I can assure you that by following it, or any of the above recommendations, you, too, can become a bad tap dancer. I know—I've tried them all.

On the danger of dancing dances

One of the outstanding results of a tour such as ours (described in Chapter 15) is the ease with which one can do the programmed dances. The show becomes a breeze, and one feels very secure. The stage is where you live—even a bad floor seems unable to mar your performance. You feel sure you have improved immensely, and you can't wait to show your friends how well you are dancing. A few days of deserved relaxation, then up to your studio to practice.

A rather unpleasant surprise awaits you. As you begin to go through the familiar pattern of warm-up and stretches at the barre and in the center, you at first feel a slight stiffness, which you attribute to the few days of layoff. It is only when the sounds of the faster steps don't sound clear, and the turns fall off even when you are undeniably warm, that you begin to reflect questioningly. Rationalization fails, and you come to the sorry conclusion that you're dancing very badly.

How can this be? You've done much more work over the past three months than you usually do. You feel fine, you've had excellent write-ups, and you weren't making any mistakes in your routines. It is this last fact that has caused the trouble. Not making mistakes is the natural result of doing the same thing over and over. You have become like a machine and a sort of automation has taken over.

As I have pointed out it is difficult to practice on the road. A short warm-up is usually all one can manage. Any practice that you do get in is on the dances that you are performing. A dance for an audience makes use of technique, often to your absolute limits, but technique is never its chief ingredient. If it were, you would be an acrobat or a juggler. Its chief ingredient is what you communicate to the audience. You do this in many ways. They are variously described by such phrases as inner drive, motor impulse, personality, tension and relaxation, artistic integrity, and other terms which strive to render into words the miracle of one person having a moving effect upon another. The point is that all these forms of telling an audience what you mean depend on the whole you—the you that you practice all your life long, not just with dance. If you work hard at making yourself skillful at this, you can be successful long after your technique has vanished (of course, you must maintain a minimal standard). Performance does not depend solely on how high your leg goes in a battement, on how cleanly you turn, or on how crisp and sparkling your tap sounds are. When you perform over and over before an audience, you learn to emphasize that about the dance which evokes the most real response. In a romantic dance this may, for instance, be the flowing quality between two sections of relatively static movement. To achieve this, you may perhaps discover that lifting your leg as high as you did in rehearsal interferes with precisely the flowing quality you want.

In a quick, fiery dance you may find that a small, nervous quality you would not allow yourself in front of a mirror creeps in to accentuate what the audience seems to like and understand best. In any case, there will inevitably be changes which are not technical, and which, in fact, relegate technique to the secondary position it should occupy in the armory of any good dancer.

The result is that when you return to class, or your own practice, where technique comes first, you will discover you haven't used certain muscles and haven't given certain neuromuscular patterns the constant work they need in order to remain patterns. In fact, if you were shown a new dance the moment you returned from a protracted tour or a long run in a hit show, you would find it much more difficult than you imagined.

I do not know of any solution to this except to make the jumps shorter on the road or cut out matinees in the city. Then you might have time to do all the things you don't do on stage. As it is, professional dancers either haven't the time or are too tired.

So if there is no practical solution to the problem, why write about it at all? It is important because it applies not only to professional dancers, who are especially affected, but also to all students and non-working dancers who spend most of their study or practice time doing routines. The ardent practice of any routine will indeed help perfect and polish that routine, and a certain amount of this is necessary, but it will also draw you away from becoming as good a dancer as you might become. It is, I admit, more fun to do a dance that you have learned and know well than it is to do exercises and single steps—particularly steps you have difficulty in doing.

There is some excuse when you have time to do only your show. There isn't any when you are free to study and practice. Although technique does play a secondary role, that role is essential, and no amount of dancing dances will keep it in shape even if the dances are very difficult. When you insist only on doing routines, you are indulging a potential frailty.

23 Improvising

Improvisation can be a most enjoyable area. And any tap dancer who has learned his basic techniques and acquired some knowledge and understanding of music and rhythm can really have a ball.

The only other ingredients necessary are a beat, an occasion, and a floor you can make a sound on. Let us assume you're standing on a floor, uncarpeted and not slippery; there's a piano and someone who can play it; and you're with friends who would like you to dance. The best thing to do is suddenly to remember that you have an important engagement with a beautiful girl. Or perhaps ask your host if he has some aspirin handy—bad tooth, headache, and all that kind of thing. The device of slipping and twisting an ankle is no longer considered advisable unless you really do it—which might hardly be worth it.

If none of these things work, you will probably have to begin to dance. Now in the very best improvisations you will be able to select a tempo and even a mood before you begin, but in the situation outlined above the man at the piano will already have started playing, and there's nothing you can do about it. If you are a young tap dancer, he will decide on *Bye Bye Blues,* and if you are, shall we say, experienced, he will probably lead off with a Chopin nocturne. Since it is unlikely that you will be able to think of a single step to do to either of these pieces, I advise you to stand in mute admiration, as if the work were so fine that you wouldn't dare intrude upon it. This usually makes the soloist sufficiently embarrassed to cut short whatever work he was engaged in, and you are right back where you started from. Given a respite, I suggest that *you* start the next time. There will be a next time, because everyone will have crowded back to give you room, and you will be standing alone in a cleared space. You'll have to dance. Now you can set a tempo you like with a strong "and 1," followed by some slaps to make your choice of tempo crystal clear. This, of course, presupposes you can make a tempo crystal clear. If you can't, you shouldn't be there. After several measures the man at the piano should have received the message and started playing in complete agreement. If he goes back to a stop-time version of the Chopin, hit him and leave the house forever. If he can play well, and does, and if he senses your mood, and you do his, then you're likely to have a great deal of pure enjoyment.

Improvisation with music is a special and secret kind of conversation between two people that is at the same time wholly exposed. You can lead and you can follow. Try to avoid clichés as you would if you were talking to someone about a subject you loved. You give and you take, and you'll sometimes find yourself doing things beyond your understanding but that come out right. Listen to the sounds you make as if they were being made by someone else. Vary the dynamics and follow your fancy—your educated fancy. Take a hint from the harmonic changes in the music. Feel as if you were developing the melody, and the melody will develop your rhythm.

Like this you can go for a long and lovely time. Like this, too, you can also court and achieve disaster. You must love where you go with an improvisation, and you must sense the whole shape of it, though the shape is yet unseen and unformed. If you can't you're likely to run into the situation where both you and the music decide to let the other have a break at the same time. You stop, the music stops, and, feeling the vacuum, you both begin in the middle of what should have been a solo phrase by one or the other of you. Sensitive, sensitive, and so very delicate is improvisation, and so very rewarding. It must finish without too much of a fight to have the last word. Some conflict is necessary, as in love, but not to the exclusion of form. To do this well you must know how long is a bar, a phrase, a chorus, or a melody. Which, of course, you should know anyhow—but which many dancers don't. You must be able to tell where the ending has to be. You either can or you can't, and if you can't—back to the drawing board, or the shoe store.

Improvisation, with all the above, can also be done without any music at all. Sometimes it's better that way. In this case, you are both the beat and the dance, and an idea or a story as well. The conversation is with yourself, and the evening should be yours. In either case, providing you have survived the initial difficulties, you should be pleasantly surprised not only by what you have learned about your dancing, but also by the very good-looking girl you hadn't noticed before and who just loves what you did. Let your own tempo begin with a strong "*and 1.*"

24 On perfection

Most dancers strive toward perfection. Western civilization has designated this goal as a proper and desirable one.

In the past whole groups have considered themselves to have reached this goal. This attitude has made subsequent generations very unhappy. To avoid this it has become an accepted fact that no group or generation may consider itself perfect. The individual, however, may continue his or her search, for even if perfection is achieved by an individual, it is not likely that it will have harmful effects on large sections of society.

The dancer is a good subject for the pursuit of this search. There are prescribed things to be done, and you can learn how to do them better and better. At a certain point you can practically say, "There, that's perfect." Moving to the field of performing, which involves creation and expression, there are still technical problems that can be assessed and practiced till they, too, are perfect.

I should like to devote the rest of this chapter to counseling against perfection, either as an achievement, or, in most cases, as something to be sought after. To judge something perfect implies that the judger is aware of some standard that is indeed without fault or blemish, something that cannot be made better. Is this standard to be measured by physical limits, and therefore to be judged differently for every different dancer's body? Or is it to be judged by some idealized image in the judger's mind? The first case would involve measurements and x-rays of such extent as to be palpably ridiculous. The second case is subject to the limited experience and recall of the individual. It might seem that there is no way to assess human perfection. For example, it can readily be determined if a singer has perfect pitch, or if an artist can draw a perfect circle. It can also be figured out if a tap dancer is keeping perfect time and making perfect rhythms. But this does not mean that the singer can sing, or the artist can draw, or the dancer can dance. It is just something about which perfection or the lack of it can be ascertained through measurement. This cannot be done in areas of creativity and expression, where the communication between performer and viewer is based upon arbitrary and subjective experience. Therefore, unless you want to dance exclusively for your mother, you cannot truly be considered perfect. And even your mother's not right.

But how about the sense of perfection you may have about yourself? This is a richer field, and of more practical use, though it, too, has many pitfalls. In this case you must make use of your own concepts of faults and blemishes, and when you have reached a state where you think you no longer have any you will at least be someplace. You may have acquired some elements of sterility in the process. The net result, however, may have some virtue. If I seem to treat this aspect of perfection-seeking rather cursorily, it is because dancers who dance for themselves alone deserve little more.

By far the most used meaning of perfection as it relates to dancers refers to the total performance. This includes everything that is needed in presenting a show—costumes, lights, music, floor surfaces, and the like.

These things, however, are often relegated to a secondary position, and the dancer concerns himself principally with the perfection of his performance—which, as we have discovered, is not subject to check. It is exactly here that the most harm can be done. Dancing is an active verb which presents itself as an individually-created means of communicating some new and vital idea to an audience. How well you function as a stimulus to that communication determines the value you have as a dancer. Trying to be perfect, either in your own terms or someone else's, can only lessen the concentration which should be devoted to evoking your predetermined images and messages. I am not advocating that you dance badly. But I do advocate that you always be fully aware of the unreal quality of perfection as it applies to dancing, and of the always real quality of yourself as you dance as beautifully as you can.

25 Suggested tap exam

Part I RHYTHM

It is customary to separate dance education into at least three categories: elementary, intermediate, and advanced. There are often innumerable sub-divisions of these three grades, and there are sometimes different teachers for each division. I think teachers should be divided according to their particular aptitude in personal relationships with students of various skills and ages rather than by the degree of technique the teachers have attained. In fact I'm not sure that it isn't advisable that a teacher of beginners have more knowledge than a teacher of advanced students. (The questions a ten-year-old can ask are really something!) In any event, I'm going to consider only two divisions— elementary and advanced—in setting the examination standards that follow. In many areas the questions will overlap, but there will be enough differences to make the divisions quite clear.

I assume an age level for beginners of at least eight or nine. In my opinion tap teachers of younger students are babysitting.

Since tap dancing deals largely with sounds that produce meaningful rhythmic patterns, the first requisite of a tap teacher should be a knowledge of rhythm and the ability to demonstrate it. This does not mean that you can count 1 a and a 2 a and a 3, etc., which may or may not indicate that you can keep time, but that you can answer the questions below, for both elementary and advanced.

1. Framework. Define: rhythm; tempo; meter; beat; accent; bar; syncopation; off beats.

2. Tools.

(a) Define: whole-notes, half-notes, quarter-notes, eighth-notes, sixteenth-notes.

(b) What does a dot after a note do to its rhythmic value?

(c) What are triplets?

(d) What are half-note, quarter-note and eighth-note triplets?

(e) What are grace notes? Demonstrate.

3. Counting.

(a) Count out loud the meter of several varied pieces of music. (To be selected by the examiner. These should include 4/4, 3/4, 3/8, 6/8, but not be of such difficulty as, for example, *Le Sacre du Printemps.* They should be from jazz, Latin American, and classical sources.)

(b) When you count the rhythm of slaps, (a 1, a 2, a 3, etc.) to which "a" are you referring—the "a" of 1 and a 2 and a 3, or the "a" of 1 a and a 2 a and a 3? Does the value change with changing tempi?

(c) How do you count thirty-second notes, and where do you use them?

(d) Count out loud the quarter notes of a piece in moderate tempo (one quarter note = 120), and perform a syncopated step while you count. Do the same while you step off the beat. Do not count the "ands."

(e) Count out loud the rhythm of half-note triplets to the same music. Do the same for quarter- and eighth-note triplets.

If you can handle the above you have sufficient knowledge of rhythm to handle most of the problems that students encounter and will ask you about in this field. If it seems too advanced and complicated, don't despair. There are many adequate teachers, and some good dancers, who know very little about rhythm. You can accomplish a great deal by just being able to keep time. But there is no question in my mind that any teacher or dancer will improve his capacity tremendously by having a thorough knowledge of rhythm. There is no substitute for the sense of security you have if you know the exact relationship of the music to the steps you are performing. It is one of the marks of distinction between animals and homosapiens. It isn't to say that there aren't many charming dancing bears and many quite musical seals. But you seldom find them in the Bolshoi Ballet or conducting a symphony.

Part II TECHNIQUE: Elementary and Intermediate

The field of tap technique has withstood all attempts at codification. Because tap has evolved from the folk forms of several cultures and has become theatrical only within the last hundred years, it has not enjoyed the long tradition necessary to give it a definitive framework. Because it has generally been performed by individuals with special gifts and has been much influenced by the personality of the individual, its technique has been dictated by the performer and not by the form. And finally, because certain parts of it can be learned by the very young and by total non-dancers, it has been considered rather as an amusing entertainment than a valid form of dance expression, and therefore not demanding of serious technical standards.

The facts leading to the development of this attitude cannot be changed, but it may be possible to develop a different attitude. With this hope I propose the tap technique examination standards that follow. As in the section on rhythm, I have not had the benefit of as much consultation with other dancers as I should like, but I have had the pleasure of having representative teachers from most sections of the country in my classes. From them I have a fair idea of existing technical standards and future potentials. I mention this to assure my readers that I do not intend to make up this examination according to my own standards, but from what appear to be reasonable goals that should be attainable by most tap teachers.

Tap technique is based on a relatively few actual sound-producing steps. Good tap dancing is based on the control, speed and smoothness with which one can perform and combine these steps, and on the movements of arms, legs and body that are incorporated with the steps.

Since there exists no accepted standardization of tap termin-
ology, where there is danger of ambiguity I have attempted to
describe the step or movement so that it will be clear even if you
know it by another name.

Basic tap technique

1. Define and demonstrate: slaps; shuffles; cramp-rolls (both
step, step, heel, heel and step, heel, step, heel—on both sides);
pull-backs (sometimes called pick-ups—what either terms means
is to stand on the ball of one foot and do a backward brush
landing either on the same or the other foot); nerve taps (this
sometimes refers to a movement performed with a rigid, tensed
leg; here it means a rapid, controlled series of foot-to-floor contacts performed with a relaxed foot); wings.

2. Demonstrate a series of steps and claps and slaps and claps
in any rhythm given by the examiner. ("Any rhythm" should be
a clearly described sequence of not longer than four bars.)

3. Perform with a steady rhythm of evenly spaced sounds (either 1 and a 2, etc., or 1 a and a 2, etc.):

  (a) Step shuffles (changing feet each step) and hop shuffles
(changing feet every two bars).

  (b) A waltz clog (done with a slap, shuffle, ball change,
slap, shuffle, ball change).

  (c) Step, shuffle, ball change, heel, slap, heel, shuffle, pull-
back (change feet), toe in back, slap heel, and into the same
combination on the other side, the last heel taking the place of
the step at the beginning of the combination.

  (d) Step, shuffle (in back), pull-back (same foot), and continue—four bars on one foot and four on the other.

4. Do any step you like at the rate of forty-eight tap sounds in
five seconds for at least ten seconds. (This reads faster than it
sounds and is not very difficult. You'll surprise yourself.) Do
the same step at the rate of twelve tap sounds in five seconds
for at least ten seconds.

5. Perform: slap R, battement L, diagonal forward, wing R, lower left leg to fifth position, step R and repeat on the other side. The rhythm is: a 1, and 2 and a 3, 4.

6. Show exercises at the barre and in the center that will strengthen the muscles used in tap dancing and develop their coordination.

7. Do a tap dance of at least two choruses in which you use syncopated on-and-off-beat rhythms and move around the floor.

You will notice that this examination is concerned with basic floor work and has no turns or jumps. These are included in the advanced examination.

Part III   TECHNIQUE: Advanced

The term "advanced" is old and worn with usage. It often means many things that bear little relationship to its original intent. Advance means to go forward or to move forward. From where and in what direction? There is a different answer for every school and every teacher, and I fear the term has long since ceased to have any real significance other than local convenience or giving a sense of pride to parents.

The setting of a tap examination in advanced technique must therefore be approached with caution. One thing, however, is clear. An advanced exam must be able to evaluate whether or not a dancer has the equipment to be a good dancer and whether or not a teacher knows how to produce and recognize one. Since there are many standards of good dancing, this puts a considerable responsibility on whoever conducts the examination. And who's going to examine the examiner? This problem has to be placed in the laps of the gods.

I think I can set down questions that will bring out what you ought to know and do to be able to dance or develop dancers, but I can't ask a question that will prove how well you apply the knowledge or do the dance. The ultimate examiner is the audience or your students. But in the hope of erecting a few beacons to light the path, here is an examination in advanced tap technique. It is assumed you have passed the first two examinations on rhythm and technique.

1. (a) Explain and discuss the rhythmic tap patterns that would be suitable for a soft-shoe, a fast 2/4, a blues, a sarabande, any two Latin American rhythms, nursery rhymes, a minuet, a waltz, an Irish jig, any jazz. Demonstrate your answers.

   (b) What is the difference between popular and classical music of the same tempo and rhythm, and how would you adapt your steps to each?

2. Do a tap dance of any length, to a tempo and rhythm you choose. Do this without music and keep strict time.

3. What is meant by rhythmic counterpoint and how does it apply to tap dancing?

In advanced technique the following questions should enable you to show that you are a good dancer or able to select one. Remember that advanced tap requires that you have some knowledge of ballet, modern, and jazz.

1. Starting on either foot, do a succession of slaps backwards and forwards. Alternate changing feet every eight counts.

2. Do a series of the following step: shuffle (in back), pull-back (change feet), toe in back, heel. Then syncopate the same in the rhythm 1 − 34 − 23.

3. Do a four-tap wing on right and left feet. (A four-tap wing means scrape out, 1; shuffle, 2,3; and land on same foot, 4.)

4. Show that you can do pirouettes (at least two, preferably three) inward and outward on both sides. Start the inward turns with a slap heel, toe in back, and a slap heel, shuffle.

5. Do jetés from side to side. Start with a brush to the side and make four sounds in landing; step, toe in back, heel, toe in back. In 3/4: 1, 2 and a 3.

6. Do a series of glissade assemblé from side to side. Make the end of the glissade step, heel, step, heel. Brush before the assemblé, and land from the assemblé in a cramp-roll (step, step, heel, heel).

7. Do a series of saute de basque. Start each one with a brush and land with a step, toe, heel, toe.

8. Do a series of wings with grand battements in moderate 3/4 time; slap R diagonal forward to left, grand battement L, wing R, slap L, diagonal forward to right, etc. (and 1 and 2 and 3). Do the same series to a fast 4/4 (and 1 and 2 and 3 and 4).

9. Do any steps you like at the rate of sixty-four taps in five seconds for at least ten seconds.

10. Do a two-chorus dance that makes use of advanced technique. Improvise one chorus to music selected by the examiner.

Note: A teacher is not expected to dance all the asked steps, but should know how they are done.

The ultimate examiner

I should like to enlarge on a thought put forward in the introduction to one of the parts of the examination. The thought is that the ultimate examiner is the audience, the student and the examiner . . . or yourself.

If this is the case, and I believe it is, why have standards at all? Why not let everyone set his own, and if these suffice within a certain community or on a certain stage, shouldn't that be sufficient? Certainly an art form of any sort is free, untrammeled, and highly individual, so why attempt to frame it within any boundaries?

I think the answer to these questions is the fact that there is no creative freedom without an accurate knowledge of limitations. Perfectly free expression usually results in chaos. Though it may be true that if you sit enough monkeys in front of enough typewriters they could eventually type all of the

Shakespeare plays and the Encyclopaedia Britannica. The chances
of a dancer reaching a similar pinnacle through random effort
are definitely not worth mentioning.

Now the building up of a personal technique to fit the apparent levels of the students in a school are not far removed
from the random effort. The accepted body of tap technique is
so small that it can easily be reached by any moderately intel-
ligent dancer. If dancers had no opportunity to discover that
there were further horizons, they could never really enjoy the
freedom of expression that is presumably theirs by virtue of
their decision to study an art form. The more clearly they become aware of real limits the more at ease they feel within them.

An examination is not something to be passed or failed, nor
is it to frustrate. It is to define the field within which you can
function and to encourage the exploration of that field. It is not
really important whether you can or can't do a four-tap wing
fluently. It is important that you know it is a tool in tap technique that you may use if you can. It isn't a serious handicap if
you can't do off-beats whenever you want to. It is a handicap
not to know that off-beats furnish a valuable means of increasing
the dramatic tension of any tap step or movement.

It is sometimes thought that teacher conventions furnish
ample new horizons and that by attending them every year you
will develop and acquire all the new material you can use. Conventions have a distinct value but they are aimed at a single
phase of dancing. They are aimed to relieve you of the very
responsibilities you should be eager to accept. In furnishing you
with material at a technical level you can easily perform, they
offer you little challenge to explore your full potential. This is
to some extent because of the limited time factor, but it is also
due to the universal desire to follow the path of least resistance.

I think that if you go over the three parts of the examination, and take all the time you need in your own studio, you
will begin a development within yourself that will prove very
valuable. You can mark yourself if you like, and work out anything that poses difficulties. You can add to it or delete whatever appears impractical for your purposes. The object is that it

will make you do the work and discover your own framework of tap dancing.

Once this is done I believe you will find a new freedom of action within which you can create more easily and inspire your students to constantly strive to surpass themselves. The passing mark is your determination to become a better dancer.

DATE DUE

GAYLORD   PRINTED IN U.S.A.